How DBT and EMDR Helped Me:

"EMDR opened a whole new chapter in my journey toward mental health. It helped lessen the strong and disturbing emotions that had been ruling my life for years. The trauma is now more of a bad memory as opposed to the daily burden it used to be. EMDR is hard work but definitely worth the commitment."
Christy C.

"When I moved to Kansas City, I immediately found the Lilac Center since they focused on Dialectical Behavior Therapy (DBT) that I found so useful for myself. I have been struggling with mental illness since I was 14 years old and can honestly say I've seen 25+ therapists, counselors, psychiatrists, psychologists, etc. throughout my years. (I've moved a lot). And at the Lilac Center, I have found the very BEST therapist I've had in my entire life. I attend individual sessions and group sessions weekly and can vouch for the change it has made in my life. If you're struggling with mental illness, or know someone that is, please consider calling the Lilac Center today. Maybe it can help you as much as it has helped me."
Kate C.

"Participating in EMDR is scary. The whole process is scary because everything is out of your control. But it allows you to move on from the things that are holding you back from living your life. It becomes your freedom."
Lindsay M.

"With EMDR, I physically felt the anxiety leave my body like a rush of water."
Laurel J.

"EMDR was like an emotional time machine that took me back to a traumatic event that made me feel horrible about myself. Using EMDR, I was able to decode the past event for what it really was, not what my mind led me to believe. Since then, EMDR has brought me back to the present and set me free so I can have a happier future."
Rachel S.

"The DBT skills can be used with all situations that you encounter in your life. The skills in this workbook help to transform you into a new person, a person who can sort through all the past trauma and live a productive and loving life. It is not an easy path but with guidance and direction you can wake up every morning knowing that particular day will be worth living. Please give this book a read and start to transform a life of misery and chaos into a life of love and peace."
Dorene P.

"Traumatic memories are a hot stove you can't keep the hand of your thoughts on. When your mind strays to these memories, it is sharply painful, and the mind reflexively withdraws. Only in allowing the mind to stay with these memories can they be reprocessed and their impact on your life eased. EMDR is a process that has gradually reduced the painful response to my own traumatic memories. This has allowed the traumatic experiences to be addressed in therapy, which in turn has improved my quality of life."
Dan B.

THIS WORKBOOK BELONGS TO:

....

A DBT AND EMDR SKILLS WORKBOOK

YOU EMPOWERED

GET BEYOND THE TRAUMA YOU'VE EXPERIENCED TO LIVE A FULL AND HAPPY LIFE

ANNA SAVIANO, MA, LPC

AMY TIBBITTS, MSW, LCSW

ISBN: 978-0-9898021-1-6
Copyright © 2014 Lilac Center LLC

Dedication

To my husband,
Your unwavering support and encouragement allows my life to
be what it is. You truly have given me everything, and allowed me
to see myself with more clarity. I am a better wife, mother, therapist
and person because of you.

To my children,
I had no idea how I could love before you. My world has more
joy and peace than I ever dreamed possible. I am inspired
by you both every day.

To my parents,
I could not be where I am were it not for the foundation of faith,
family, and unconditional love you gave me. I strive to pass
on that legacy.

To my clients,
Your tears and laughter, willfulness and radical honesty are
truly awesome. I am honored to be a small part of your life and
healing journey.

-Anna

Table of Contents

quick find: Worksheets and Exercises

DISCLAIMER

This book is meant as a resource to help you learn about Dialectical Behavior Therapy (DBT) and Eye Movement Desensitization & Reprocessing (EMDR) skills to help with reducing trauma responses. This book is not a replacement for diagnosis and treatment from a professional licensed Therapist. We encourage you to seek out professional help and attend individual and group therapy from a DBT and/or EMDR provider.

LILAC CENTER: *who we are*

Kansas City, Mo.,-based Lilac Center is the premier provider of Dialectical Behavior Therapy services in the greater Kansas City metro and surrounding area.

Lilac Center has successfully provided a wide range of psychological services with a Dialectical Behavior Therapy (DBT) and Eye Movement Desensitization & Reprocessing (EMDR) focus. DBT teaches problem-solving techniques designed to foster a healthy balance in thoughts, feelings and actions. EMDR assists with reducing trauma responses and being fully present.

This workbook was developed by Anna Saviano, MA, LPC and Amy Tibbitts MSW, LCSW, director of Lilac Center. After developing the *You Untangled* workbook and seeing the success our clients experienced using it, we decided to develop the next step in helping our clients in their journey of recovery.

This is that next step. Once you have mastered the skills taught in Dialectical Behavior Therapy, you have the stability to dig deeper within and heal from the core trauma you've experienced.

The exercises taught in this book can bring about strong emotional feelings and reactions. We strongly encourage you to seek help from a professional in your area as you work through this material.

For a refresher on DBT Skills taught in *You Untangled,* consider joining our companion website: *mydbtgroup.com.* It includes videos of group sessions teaching the DBT skills found in this series of books. The website also includes worksheets and additional resources about Borderline Personality Disorder and Dialectical Behavior Therapy. Many of our clients have found *mydbtgroup.com* to be very helpful in learning DBT and better understanding the skills in this book. We hope you will too.

Congratulations on taking steps to build a happy, healthy, fulfilling life!

Lilac Center

- ⓘ www.lilaccenter.org
- 👤 www.mydbtgroup.com
- ⓕ facebook.com/lilaccenter
- ⓥ @lilaccenter

ACKNOWLEDGMENTS

Thank you to Marsha Linehan, for giving the world Dialectical Behavior Therapy. Without this amazing therapy, countless individuals would remain in perpetual conflict. Thank you for sharing your personal story and instilling hope for those who struggle.

Much gratitude to Francine Shapiro for sharing her experiences and the development of EMDR. Without this tool, this therapy would not be possible. Thank you to all the consultants, trainers and fellow therapists who have shared resources, techniques and support. The EMDR community's collaborative and industrious nature is truly inspirational and motivational.

Anna Saviano, MA, LPC

Amy Tibbitts, MSW, LCSW

introduction
USING THIS WORKBOOK

You're reading this workbook because you have completed the work in *You Untangled*, and are ready for the next step in your recovery journey.

You have extinguished your self-harm behavior and have learned to implement DBT skills routinely in your daily life. However, you may still experience trauma reactions based on unresolved issues from your past. If that is the case, you are in the right place.

In this workbook, we will explore trauma, which is at the root of Borderline Personality Disorder and many other emotional problems.

Trauma responses can have a pervasive impact, keeping your mind overwhelmed with fear and stuck in negative beliefs. You may struggle with keeping current and past issues separate. It's possible that you have difficulty internalizing positive experiences or believing good things are possible for you.

Whether you are working through this book alone, or with a therapist as part of your treatment, we hope that you will find the principles and exercises clear and practical.

This may be your first exposure to trauma processing in a workbook format. It is critical to seek a trained EMDR therapist if material surfaces that is too intense to manage on your own.

That's not always possible, so the next best option, in our opinion, is to work with therapists who can provide trauma-informed treatment and who are willing to help you stabilize and process information.

If you are currently without access to a mental health treatment provider, you can still benefit greatly from this workbook, particularly as you determine to stay the course of practice.

Commit to yourself to learn and apply the exercises, and you will find yourself becoming more insightful, grounded and present. You will be able to observe the past without getting swept up by it, and recognize the impact it has on your current life.

This workbook will provide concepts, tools and exercises to help you resolve past trauma. You will begin to make important changes that give you more control over yourself and will help you thrive in the long term.

If you are suffering, there is hope; things can and do get better.

The clients we have seen with repeated trauma responses have become unstuck, gained understanding and compassion for themselves, and parted ways with the shame cycle of trauma reactions.

They have built lives congruent with their values and relationships that are healthy and strong.

There is no promise in therapy, but there is hope for change. Research confirms that the skills you learned in the first workbook, combined with engagement in insight work, helps alleviate symptoms of Borderline Personality Disorder and Post-Traumatic Stress Disorder. Our goal is for you to rediscover hope through using this book.

It is important you remain strong and competent in your everyday life. Practice the DBT skills you learned in *You Untangled* and be careful not to get lost in past trauma. Remember you have created a life worth living for yourself now.

Oftentimes when people live their whole lives reacting to their trauma and trying to run away from awareness, they have forgotten that they are **fully capable of facing life**. We consider learning Dialectical Behavior Therapy skills to be stage one trauma work because you are learning to live life on life's terms. Stage two is exploring and understanding this trauma and the subsequent trauma responses. This understanding will help you feel more compassion for yourself and others.

Before you can fully understand your past, you must be present.

To be present, you cannot be constantly reacting emotionally, dissociating and remaining caught up in addiction cycles with food, sex, drugs, spending, gambling or intense relationship chaos. Dialectical Behavior Therapy provides the skills needed to manage your emotions, relationships and distress in effective ways to create a rewarding life.

Exploring your past and then understanding your trauma responses can be very therapeutic but can only be done when you can maintain a dual reality. In other words, you must recognize that the past affects your present moments, but **the past does not define your present**. You must realize you have power over your responses and that you are not powerless against your emotions. You need a strong skills base to leave the past in the past and return to a healthy, happy life. During the process of working through the workbook, reach out to a licensed therapist for assistance, especially if you feel overwhelmed.

This will be an exciting journey and you will develop deep understanding, compassion and a newfound respect for yourself through completing this workbook. Your relationships will be healthier and with help, you will come to see your life as a gift. Sometimes the challenges we must endure can impart the greatest rewards.

forward

MOVING BEYOND THE PAST

By Anna Saviano, MA, LPC

*"The curious paradox is that when I **accept** myself just as I am, then I can **change**."* — Carl Rogers

I began my clinical work with people who had been impacted by sexual violence. I was straight out of graduate school, and had all the enthusiasm and energy of a young professional. I was going to help people! I was (and still am) optimistic, hopeful and hard working. Life began to catch up, though, and I felt in a rut.

At that time, I began to really define my professional orientation. In school, they push this. And everyone says *eclectic.*

But how could you choose just one theory to go by? Doesn't it need to be based on the individual you're working with?

In short, the answer is "yes." However, as I have come to learn, almost everyone who seeks counseling has experienced some form of trauma, abuse or otherwise maladaptive life experience. It is through this lens that I have developed my personal approach.

I have been fortunate to work with amazing professionals and mentors. As a result, I have participated in various training opportunities.

Through my work with sexual abuse survivors, I was able to begin and see the direction my professional path would take.

The resilience, dedication and hard work I saw was remarkable. The human mind, body and spirit are truly incredible. Individuals were able to move beyond their past, and participate fully in life *as it happens.*

Isn't that what we all strive for? To live our lives fully, free of weight from the past and able to be present?

I believe that we are all seeking peace, and this is what drives us.

For individuals with Borderline Personality Disorder (BPD), this journey can be particularly daunting. If you have sought peace, but have found little, this workbook may be for you. If you have struggled to leave the past behind, and participate fully in life on life's terms, then this book is definitely for you. Peace *is* within your reach.

To that end, I have found the most useful resources in therapy to be Dialectical Behavior Therapy (DBT) and Eye Movement Desensitization and Reprocessing (EMDR).

The combination of the daily skills taught in DBT provides structure, form and the value of acceptance. Through skills training, I have seen individuals go from living a reactive and chaotic life to living one of peace and stability. Daily functioning is significantly improved.

The dialectical dilemma of acceptance and change, which is explored in DBT, permeates life at all levels. We are constantly challenged to consider both options, and DBT provides the framework for navigating those challenges.

It is my belief that individuals who experience such difficulty in daily living are not responding only to the events that are currently happening. These folks are reacting to the present based on the past.

Maybe you are aware of how this presents in your life, or maybe you only suspect that you are not living in the moment. In either case, EMDR can likely be helpful to you.

What is driving your current actions and emotions? Are you holding onto a negative belief from the past and finding all the proof to back it up in the present?

EMDR can help sort through these beliefs, past events, and associated emotional and bodily sensations. Through addressing the past issues, I have seen the true peace and resilience of self emerge. When we tune into our body and mind, we are more readily able to participate wholly in the moment.

It is my hope for you, the reader and participant in *your* life, to find peace within yourself.

To grow and learn and develop your true good nature, and **live fully in your mind and body**, is the most valuable gift you can give yourself.

Chapter 1

WHAT IS TRAUMA?

"I am not afraid of storms, for I am learning how to sail my ship."

Louisa May Alcott

Trauma limits us from expressing who we are and from living life fully.

Living a life with energy and openness is shadowed by the trauma (or for some,

multiple traumas). Trauma separates what belongs together and attaches

what does not belong together. Oftentimes, the intensity of the fears associated

with the events cannot be understood, processed nor internalized. Some people

are left with a shaken or broken core, and a lost sense of well-being. In this

chapter, we will explore the definition of trauma and define the psychological

distress that can impair functioning.

WHAT IS TRAUMA?

Trauma is often defined in a limiting and sometimes invalidating way. Francine Shapiro, the creator of EMDR (Eye Movement Desensitization and Reprocessing), has expanded this definition based on current research and clinical experience.

It is important to understand what can be referred to as a trauma, and how such events impact development and daily living.

In Francine Shapiro's initial introduction of EMDR, she referred to "big T" and "little t" trauma. These categories have been broadened and are generally referred to as "maladaptive life experiences."

Through this new lens, we are able to include a multitude of events which may have a lasting impact on an individual's functioning but not meet traditional criteria for trauma. If you have been diagnosed with PTSD or believe that a traumatic event(s) is impacting your current functioning, then EMDR may work for you. We'll look at information processing systems and this will help determine what, from your past, may be pushing your current life.

WHAT IS PTSD?

Post-Traumatic Stress Disorder (PTSD) may seem like a relatively simple concept at first. Most people associate combat, sexual assault and natural disasters with PTSD.

However, as we see with PTSD and Complex PTSD (C-PTSD), psychological distress can result from more than just the traumas that make our headlines.

Whatever the event(s) may have been, it is likely that they have caused significant impairment in your social interactions, capacity to work, or other important areas of functioning. Assess yourself using the following list of symptoms.

RE-EXPERIENCING

• Do you have intrusive memories of past events?
• Do you experience dreams related to stressful events?
• Do you experience flashbacks?
• Do you experience intense emotional or physical distress when exposed to reminders of the event?

AVOIDANCE

- Do you avoid any thoughts about the events(s)?
- Do you try to stuff emotions that come up?
- Are there places or people that you avoid?

NEGATIVE COGNITIONS AND MOOD

- Do you experience thinking problems, particularly related to the past?
- Do you blame others or yourself?
- Are you experiencing decreased interest in activities?
- Do you have pieces missing from your memory?

AROUSAL

- Do you engage in any reckless or self-destructive behavior?
- Is your sleep disturbed?
- Are you hyper-aware of your surroundings?

You may also experience dissociation. This can occur if you experience depersonalization or derealization.

DEPERSONALIZATION

- Do you ever feel as though you are watching yourself from the outside?
- Does the world ever seem vague or like a dream, as if things are not real or important?

DEREALIZATION

- Does the world ever seem flat or colorless, lacking depth?
- Do you ever feel as though the world does not seem real?

According to NAMI, the National Alliance on Mental Illness, PTSD is diagnosed in roughly 10 percent of women and 5 percent of men in their lifetime. Many others will experience the adverse effects of trauma in their lives. PTSD is a response to events that threaten injury to self or others and includes persistent fear, helplessness or horror. This also includes being a witness to or victim of sexual abuse or domestic violence.

WHAT IS C-PTSD?

Complex Post-Traumatic Stress Disorder (C-PTSD) is not currently an official diagnosis. However, it has been researched and documented in a wide array of articles and books on the subject of trauma and stress related problems.

C-PTSD is a psychological injury resulting from ongoing exposure to social and/or interpersonal trauma in the context of "captivity" (a situation from which the victim cannot reasonably escape, e.g. childhood). If you grew up in an invalidating or chaotic environment, that could lead to C-PTSD. The outcome of this could include feeling out of control and helpless. You may also struggle with knowing yourself, and feeling connected to yourself. [1, 2, 3]

In the first book of this series, *You Untangled*, Borderline Personality Disorder is discussed in-depth. You learned that it is the result of a combination of an invalidating environment and a predisposition to emotional sensitivity. Marsha Linehan explained this with her biosocial theory.

Complex PTSD can also be a result of this type of upbringing. It is certainly an invalidating environment in which sexual abuse, domestic violence and/or neglect are allowed to take place.

People who experience chronic trauma often report additional symptoms alongside formal PTSD symptoms, such as changes in their self-perception and the way they adapt to stressful events.

Consider the following questions to assess yourself. If you answer "yes" to these questions, you should consider working through the workbook with your therapist to assist you with maintaining awareness.

- Are you consistently feeling depressed?
- Have you been thinking about suicide?
- Are you frequently angry or do you have uncontrollable anger outbursts?
- Do you lack memories of your childhood?
- Does it feel like you are reliving a traumatic event?
- Do you feel detached from your life, or who you are (everything feels unreal)?
- Do you have aggressive or homicidal thoughts toward your offender or others?
- In your relationships, do you ever find yourself in the role of the caregiver but not trusting others to give you care?
- In your relationships, do you repeatedly search for a rescuer?
- Do you feel hopeless despair and an inability to find meaning in life?
- Do you feel the past trauma has total power over you and obsess over the events?

If these apply to you, then the exercises in this book will be helpful. We will look at how these areas have been affected by your own trauma, and what steps can be taken to put the past behind you and start living a mindful, connected life. EMDR can be a critical part of treatment for PTSD and C-PTSD.

Chapter 2

KEY CONCEPTS OF EMDR

"The eyes are the window to your soul."

William Shakespeare

In the following chapter, you will learn the theory and key concepts of Eye Movement Desensitization & Reprocessing (EMDR). This type of therapy has proven successful in reprocessing memories in those impacted by trauma. You will learn how the brain processes trauma and how EMDR promotes change.

THE THEORY OF EMDR

Francine Shapiro developed EMDR in order to help people who had experienced traumatic events. The way that she understood trauma to impact the brain was through the idea of information processing.

Our brain and body take in a ton of information every day. We are constantly, if not consciously, sorting through this information and keeping what is needed and getting rid of the rest. Ideally, we are able to adapt to our surroundings and shift our thought processes as needed.

Unfortunately, this is not always the case. If you experienced routine trauma in your childhood, your system may have become overloaded. In this situation, your brain and body did the best they could, but may have developed some maladaptive or unhelpful strategies and belief systems as a result.

For example, if you are teased at school, it is likely that you are able to let go of that if you have a supportive family and stable network of friends and the teasing does not become a major issue.

However, if you are teased, and your mom wants to know what you did to deserve it, and you don't really have other friends, then you might come to doubt your self-worth.

From that experience, then, you start to pay extra attention to other situations that make you feel this way. Our brain has a tricky way of working in this regard; we like to be right, so we end up paying special attention to whatever proves our belief. Shapiro described this as networking, so that experiences that are similar end up linked together. That's great if you have a lot of positive life experiences that link up in a network around feeling safe or loved. It's not so great when the network has feeling worthless or unloved at its core.

If the negative events keep happening, the information processing we talked about earlier is interrupted. Strong negative feelings or dissociation (disconnecting from your body or environment) can interfere with processing.

While those feelings and dissociation may have made sense at the time, or even been helpful to keep you safe, they keep your brain from adapting to what has happened. Connections aren't made with healthy networks, so traumatic material is stored in the parts of the brain for emotions and body sensations.

Consider this example. A sexual assault survivor may "know" that rapists are responsible for the crime, but this knowledge does not connect with her feelings that she is to blame.

The memory is then dysfunctionally stored without appropriate connections and with many elements still unprocessed. Having knowledge does not automatically impact our emotions. This is also the foundation for flashbacks or intrusive memories. When someone thinks about their trauma, or is prompted to by a trigger, they may feel like they are reliving it, and/or experience strong emotions and physical sensations.

This results in PTSD or C-PTSD.

You may need to take a break at this point. Remember the DBT skills you learned in the previous book *You Untangled*. There are other opportunities throughout this workbook that will help you remain present in the moment and tolerate stress. Access these as needed.

It is important for you to know that all kinds of events can be maladaptively processed and stored, leading to trauma responses, PTSD or C-PTSD. It is not only major, life-threatening events that cause problems.

When seemingly small events happen and you feel like you *should* respond better, remember how information processing works. It could be that a network is being tapped that you're unaware of, and your emotional response is based not just on the immediate event, but on the past, as well. Remember to be gentle with yourself as you explore what kind of traumatic experiences you may have had, and how they could have been processed.

For people who have experienced multiple or long-term traumas, "disproportionate responses" often occur.

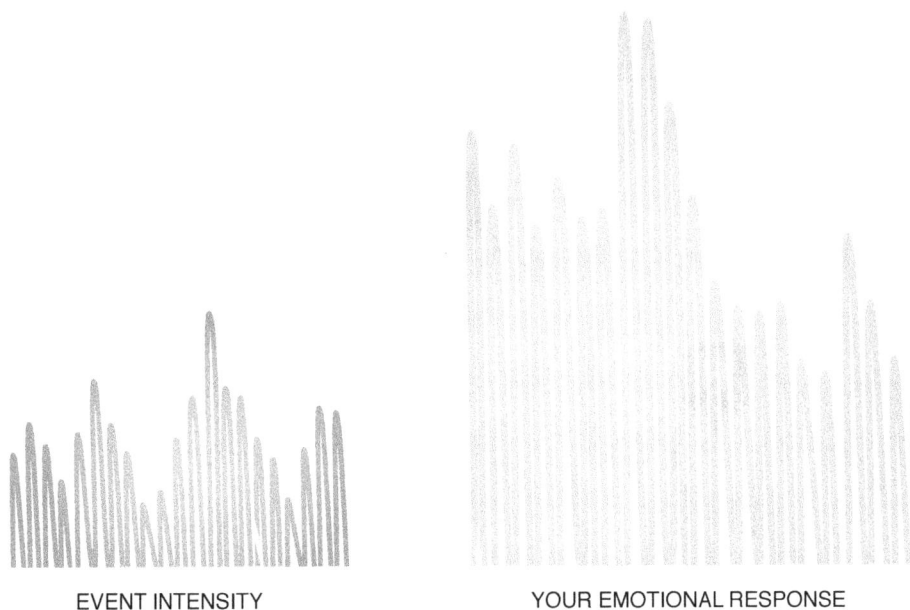

EVENT INTENSITY   YOUR EMOTIONAL RESPONSE

This is when an event occurs that may be ranked on a scale of 1 to 10 at a 2 or 3, but you respond with the intensity of a 7 or 8. When this happens, it is likely that maladaptively stored past information is being tapped into.

Many clients are able to identify this but struggle to manage their emotional response. DBT skills can help with this, and EMDR can help resolve the underlying issues contributing to your disproportionate response. Use the scale on the next page to understand how you rank events in your life and determine if it is proportionate.

✏ Exercise:

RANK THE INTENSITY OF YOUR DISTRESS

• Is your intensity in proportion with the event?

• Do you find yourself at the high end of distress often?

• Have people suggested that your response is more intense than a situation calls for?

Think of distressing events in your life and identify where they fall on the scale. It is helpful in gaining perspective on your intensity. If everything feels like severe distress, you may be misinterpreting things and past trauma could be to blame.

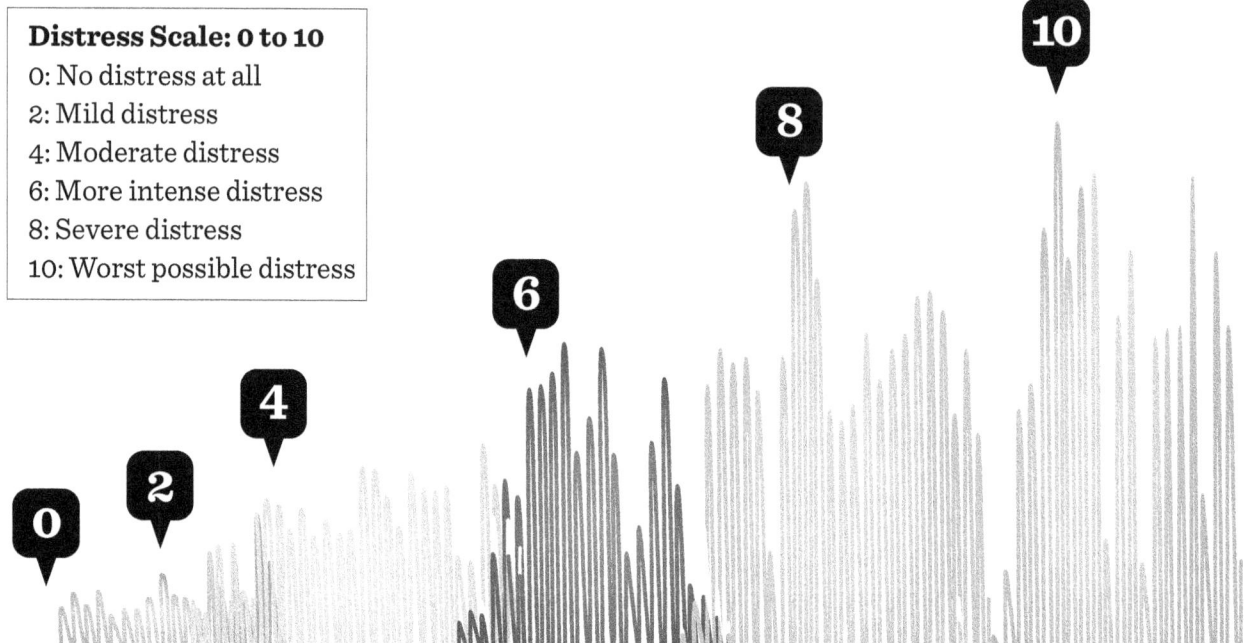

Distress Scale: 0 to 10
0: No distress at all
2: Mild distress
4: Moderate distress
6: More intense distress
8: Severe distress
10: Worst possible distress

Information processing is the key to alleviating the symptoms brought on by trauma. It is believed that when a memory is targeted for reprocessing, it is then linked up with more adaptive information. Learning takes place, and the negative network is broken down. The experience is stored with appropriate emotions and beliefs. Something that was previously highly-charged will be more easily and less painfully recalled after reprocessing.

Research

Originally intended for work with PTSD, EMDR has also been shown to be effective with multiple other disorders including generalized anxiety disorder, social phobia, body dysmorphia, anger dyscontrol, marital discord, personality and attachment disorders, depression and existential angst.

EMDR research is a robust and quickly growing field. Increasingly, EMDR is being used to address issues related to C-PTSD and attachment. We will also explore how EMDR and resolution of past hurts can help decrease symptoms of BPD and increase quality of life for you.

KEY CONCEPTS

AIP (ADAPTIVE INFORMATION PROCESSING)

This is the theory of how information is processed and stored in our brains, as we discussed previously. When events are not processed effectively because they are too big, repetitive or damaging, they become stored maladaptively.

When this processing system does not function properly, a touch, look, emotion or situation can link into the unprocessed network and trigger emotions or physical sensations that are part of the trauma. These are the memories that are intrusive and can be disruptive to daily living. You might experience this as a flashback or trigger.

BLS (BILATERAL STIMULATION)

Bilateral stimulation (BLS) refers to the alternate stimulation used in EMDR reprocessing and that can also be used to manage minor anxieties on your own. Bilateral means that you are alternating between the right and left side. It can include tapping on knees or shoulders, sounds, eye movements, or handheld "buzzies" applied in an alternating pattern. Although it is not certain what the underlying mechanism is that makes this effective, as with many forms of psychotherapy, there are some theories.

One possible reason that BLS works is that it sets off a relaxation response. Consider the soothing feeling of rocking, which may go back to the prenatal experience of being lulled while in utero. It may stimulate the body system in charge of rest and relaxation (parasympathetic nervous system).

Another possibility is the similar physical experience of BLS to REM sleep. During sleep, information is processed adaptively and the day's events are resolved. BLS may simulate this by forcing attention to shift across the middle of the brain and therefore adaptively process it. It is likely that ongoing research will continue to provide answers.

The bilateral stimulation most often used independently is tapping, either as the butterfly hug or knee tapping. This allows you to practice on your own and experience the relaxing effects of BLS. There are worksheets that illustrate how to practice these skills on your own.

DUAL AWARENESS

Another key feature of EMDR is that of dual awareness. This refers to the practice of maintaining awareness of the current situation while looking at the past. We do not want to re-experience the past; rather, we want to place attention on it while allowing our brains to process and adaptively store information from past events. This is a perfect opportunity to practice mindfulness strategies.

Take a moment to consider how easily you are able to move back and forth between thinking about past events and what is going on in this moment. This is a skill worth developing, as it is crucial to processing traumatic material. I encourage you to practice this often, not just when working on traumatic memories.

THREE-PRONGED APPROACH

In addition to dual awareness and BLS, EMDR promotes a three-pronged approach. This means that the first priority is to resolve past events and trauma.

The next step is to address current situations that may be linked to the same networks. What in your current life is connected to the past?

Finally, future events are imagined so that you can acquire whatever new skills you may need to deal with them. In the example of a sexual assault victim, the first priority would be to address the memories of the event itself. Next, the target would be anything in everyday life that is triggering, such as places or sounds. Finally, thinking about going on dates, walking alone, or being around men in the future would be addressed so that the entire network has been processed.

You won't forget about past trauma or stress, but it will cease to cause an emotional response in your daily functioning.

NEUROBIOLOGY

This section will explain how neurobiology factors into trauma response.

The Neurobiology of Trauma

People are programmed to respond to threats to their safety. Unfortunately, this set of adaptive responses in the face of terror, which are lifesaving in the moment, can leave people with ongoing, long-term psychological symptoms. The biological mechanisms that encourage the powerful and protective "fight or flight" response and maximize physical safety at the time, such as enabling a woman to fight off an attacker during a sexual assault, can create complex problems later.

When faced with terror, less critical body functions (e.g., the parts of the brain where memory, emotion and thinking are processed) get "turned off" in the service of immediate physical safety.

Specifically, this "fight or flight" response increases the heart rate, moves more blood to muscles and adds stress hormones to help fight off infection and bleeding in case of a wound. As a result, the traumatic experiences are not processed at the time they happen because the body is focusing entirely on immediate physical safety.

A poorly integrated traumatic experience can be unpredictable and unexpected. The unprocessed memories of a traumatic event can occur without warning.

Experiencing traumatic events can change the way our brains function. As long as thoughts, memories and feelings associated with the trauma remain disconnected from the actual event, it is difficult for people living with PTSD to access their inner experiences because the normal flow of emotion remains deeply affected by the traumatic event. This can keep a person stuck in a pattern that may induce anxiety, sleeplessness, anger or increased risk for self-harming behavior.

Compelling neuroscience research has shown that activity in the brain actually moves after reprocessing through EMDR.

Prior to reprocessing, individuals who are thinking about their trauma show lots of activity in the area of the brain associated with vision. Following reprocessing, activity shifts to the more language-oriented region of the brain. The traumatic material becomes part of the "story" but is no longer distressing when recalled.

Before	**After EMDR sessions**

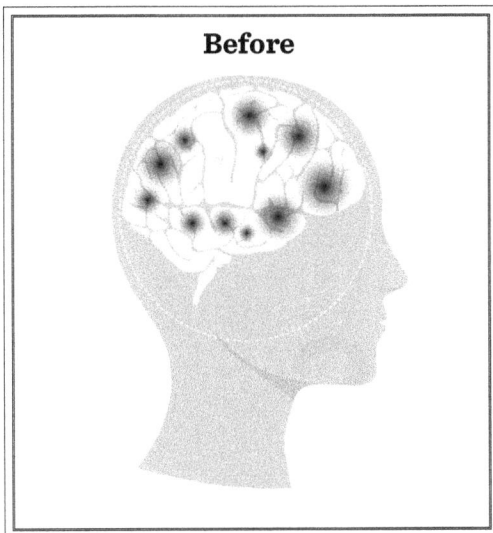

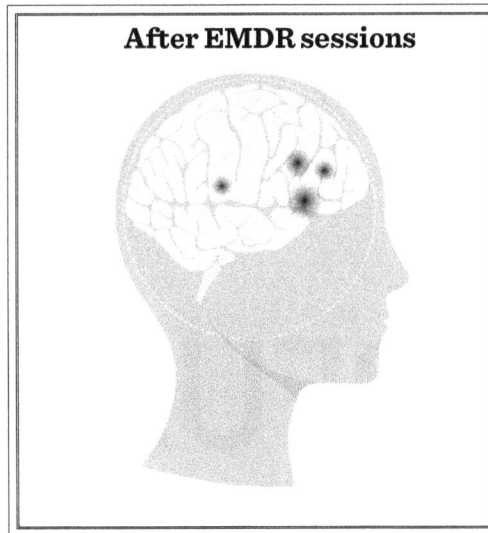

IMAGES ARE SIMULATION ONLY

EMDR And The Effects On The Brain

Brain scans of a woman with Post-Traumatic Stress Disorder done after four 90-minute EMDR sessions show a dramatic decrease in overactivity in the brain. See actual brain scans by Dr. Daniel Amen at *www.amenclinics.com/the-science/spect-gallery*.

✳ *in* Summary

- Similar experiences are linked together in memory networks
- During traumatic events it is common to disconnect from your body or environment
- This disconnect prevents your brain from making healthy connections
- Negative beliefs about yourself and maladaptive associations are common
- Extra attention is given to whatever proves our beliefs, even if the belief is negative and incorrect
- People move through time proving to themselves the negative beliefs that they formed out of trauma events

EMDR offers a way to gain insight as to when your negative beliefs and associations formed, and to evaluate the accuracy of the beliefs. For example:

- Mary currently has few friends
- She was left alone and neglected as a child
- She believes if people really got to know her, they would not want to be around her
- Therefore, she shies away from being open in relationships
- She spends time frequently recalling the few times she was open and how it backfired with judgment and criticism

Through EMDR, Mary may be able to challenge beliefs about herself and develop a sense that her parents' neglect was not her fault.

Chapter 3

MINDFULNESS IN PRACTICE

"It's not a matter of letting it go — you would if you could. Instead of 'let it go,' we should probably say 'let it be.'"

Jon Kabat-Zinn

Remember, the goal of mindfulness is to become purposeful in how you are living your life by increasing your awareness and to reduce suffering by being fully present. This is wisdom; let it guide you. Your inner wisdom will allow the true meaning and purpose of your life to shine. In the following chapter, you will practice mindfulness exercises, the core skill necessary for living a fulfilling life.

LIVING IN YOUR LIFE: WHAT IS MINDFULNESS?

Mindfulness is the core skill in DBT. You might think of it as a center of a bicycle wheel, with the other skills being the spokes all converging and intersecting there at the center. You will need mindfulness to become increasingly effective with the other skills. When you practice crisis survival skills, emotion regulation or relationship skills, the more mindful you are, the more effective you will be.

Mindfulness, which can be described in a thousand ways, is at the very least, a practice in paying attention. It's about **expanding your awareness** to your experiences, your emotions, your behaviors and your thoughts. Even the world around you, the things you long for, and the things you fear.

Mindfulness can also be described as seeing, truly seeing with clarity; seeing things as they are without necessarily trying to change them.

As you begin your practice of mindfulness, you may see more vividly the clutter of your mind's racing thoughts, self-condemnation and impulsive behaviors. You may also see more clearly your own vision for what you want your life to look like: free of emotional suffering, connected in **secure relationships**, and free from the tyranny of impulsivity.

Mindfulness is about living in or with yourself, even becoming more genuinely interested in yourself and your own life. We might even say mindfulness helps you to be at home with yourself.

Mindfulness practice addresses problems with dissociation, or that experience of zoning out. You don't have to "check out" when you face stressful situations, even though that may be a pattern for you at this moment. If that's the case, then that's the case. We simply have to accept that.

But since dissociation creates problems in memory, learning and effective engagement with your life, it must change.

Mindfulness helps you to develop increased tolerance for your strong emotions. Mindfulness won't make your emotions less strong, but your practice will move you closer to allowing your primary emotional responses to be what they are: normal and fundamentally adaptive.

As you practice simply **noticing** your emotional responses without complicating them with judgments or non-acceptance, you will perhaps begin to see them anew as friends that provide you with motivation, and with information about things going on around you. They can also assist you in connecting in relationships.

Your practice of these mindfulness skills will help untangle complicated thoughts: the judgments, the self-invalidation, and the exaggerations of either/or thinking as you discover that many of the "shoulds" you have come to believe in are conditioned assumptions that don't always square with the facts. If you let yourself, you will come to disbelieve many misconceptions about yourself: "I shouldn't be so sensitive," "I should just suck it up," "I should always have it all together."

In your practice of mindfulness, you will just notice these thoughts, simply see them without acting on them, and perhaps with some regularity challenge them with questions such as, "Well, why shouldn't I be so sensitive?" "Why should I just suck it up?" and "Why should I have it all together, and what does that really mean anyway?"

Mindfulness, as applied to your behaviors, will help you see more clearly situations where you are more vulnerable to impulsivity, and the experience of impulse urges rising up inside of you when you become agitated, frightened or lonely.

Just seeing these urges without reacting to them can provide you with some space to choose alternate courses of actions, perhaps turning toward exercise, music, reading, prayer and other activities instead.

Just noticing your self-destructive behaviors, factually and without judgment, allows you to see patterns of triggers, behaviors and their consequences, and you can better evaluate them as effective or ineffective, and have better information about how to effectively change them with specific behavioral plans, rather than getting bogged down in judgments about them.

Mindfulness in relationships can lead you to fuller enjoyment of loved ones and friends, as you bring your **full self**, with all of your attention, to a delicious meal, discussion over tea, or play with a child. Having presence in these moments, without becoming distracted by worry, or thoughts like, "I don't deserve this," "When will the storm return?" or "I'm still miserable," can make it possible for you to just drink in the experience of fun, happiness or joy.

Mindfulness in relationships will help you increase your tolerance for the foibles and fallibility of other people. You can simply notice that your friend is 10 minutes late without assuming that they're blowing you off; you can simply notice the fear of rejection come and go, without reacting to it; you can accept the apologies of others who attempt to repair their relationship when they have let you down.

Mindfulness in relationships will help you to express how you feel toward others effectively, whether an expression of love, or an expression of disappointment when they let you down.

LIVING INTO YOUR LIFE: PRACTICING MINDFULNESS

To live at home with yourself, to relinquish rigid demands on yourself and others, to change your focus from fear and self-loathing, you will have to practice. You will have to practice **simply noticing your emotions**, thoughts and behaviors without reacting to them, or without, as some mindfulness teachers say, attaching to them. You begin by simply noticing these things, just seeing them, and watching them, without applying either/or judgments.

MINDFULNESS AS MIND CONTROL

Mindfulness is both simple and difficult. It is simple when you consider that you carry with you at all times the necessary equipment for the practice. That is, you have yourself, and we will explain this a bit more in a moment.

On the other hand, mindfulness is difficult to practice because of the well-conditioned patterns of thought you hold. For all your life, you have been taught to think in categories of either/or, and "should" about everything. If you hold a fundamental belief that you should be able to solve all of your problems on your own, and you find that you can't do it on your own, you feel terrible for violating the "should."

If you believe other people should always, in every situation, give you what you want, and they don't, you feel terrible about them for not doing what they should. If you believe you should just ignore your negative emotions, but you can't, because you experience them regardless of your beliefs, you will think of yourself as a failure, which in turn may trigger a downward spiral into feeling even worse.

Mindfulness is also difficult to practice when you consider our go-go-go world. There is so much noise and clutter, entertainment and enticements to get more, be beautiful, drive this car, stuff and things are the key to happiness, and so on. We have many conveniences that encourage us to do more in a single instant than what is hardly possible.

Given these factors, it's no wonder that the practice of mindfulness, as we have described it so far, and the exercise you are about to read about and practice, can seem strange, or sound so impossible.

Reactive thinking, the ebb and flow of anxiety, want and the demands of our multitask world, keep us from awareness. Often the thoughts are contradictory or confused; we vacillate between extremes.

Mindfulness is a practice of bringing your attention under your control, to soothe the mind and to simplify the activity of your thoughts.

MINDFULNESS BASICS

The following principles are the basics that will guide and shape your practice of mindfulness.

BREATHE

Breathing is fundamental to the practice of mindfulness. In every tradition of mindfulness, whatever its root, breathing is key to becoming centered, calm and attentive.

What do we mean by breathe?

We mean changing the path of breath from your normal breathing, which is likely shallow and primarily in the upper portion of your lungs, to the more natural path through the diaphragm and through the lower portion of your lungs for more breath, deeper breath. Singers, well-trained public speakers, actors and practitioners of the martial arts, yoga and meditation all know the power of breathing from the diaphragm.

NOTICE

We have already gone on at some length about noticing or seeing. With respect to your practice of mindfulness, we ask you to practice, through these exercises, **noticing what you feel**, **noticing what you think**, **noticing what you do**, and **what you *want* to do**, or what urges you feel toward action. This noticing will become a practice in knowing what you feel, think, do and what to do.

DESCRIBE

At this step of your practice, we ask you to describe what you notice in factual terms rather than with judgmental labels.

For example, when you notice that you feel angry, practice saying to yourself, "I feel anger." You can see the simplicity in that, and you may already see the complexity, too. At first you may want to express judgments about why you're feeling angry, perhaps wanting to say instead, "My boss is such a jerk, he never treats me fairly. I should quit my job. He makes me so mad."

Judgments are well-conditioned, so it will be a difficult practice, but not impossible.

ENGAGE WITH PRESENCE

Your practice of mindfulness is not about sitting cross-legged in a dark room repeating mantras, or fantasizing about a life you can't have. Although, as you soon find, there are some exercises for learning and increasing your skills that require you to withdraw from your normal activities to practice and to recollect yourself when your thoughts and emotions and energies are scattered about.

This practice of mindfulness will also help you cultivate the life you want by participating in your life, in each moment as it comes, facing each situation as it is as skillfully as you can at that moment. Rather than avoid situations through dissociation, not having conversations that are painful or not changing behavioral patterns, you will approach them with new tools, and find that you can develop increasing tolerance for difficult tasks, situations and even your own painful emotions. This also requires that you are present for your life, even in difficult situations.

ONE THING

Part of your practice will be to **engage in one thing at a time**, rather than trying to engage everything at once, which is difficult and often overwhelming.

You will practice simplifying how you approach your relationships, behaviors and other tasks, making things easier on yourself.

This element of mindfulness is the practice of selecting what you pay attention to in a given moment, or how you will focus.

To stay focused, or concentrated, will require that you choose what activity, situation, thoughts or emotions you focus on, and in turn, that which you can become more selective and deliberate about what you choose to do, and where your mind goes.

Ironically, the more you slow down, the more deliberate and focused you are, the more you get done. You're likely to get more done because you will be able to prioritize tasks, and do them with increased efficiency and fewer mistakes.

✏️ Exercise One:
AWARENESS AND ATTENTION TO YOUR BREATH

Instructions: Read the description of each exercise and then practice. Remember, you're not in a contest, no one is keeping track of whether or not you do this right; this is just practice. Each time you practice one of these exercises you will become a little more proficient at it.

If you begin your practice and find your mind goes all over the place or leaves your practice, just notice that you're off-course, and that your mind has wandered. And then gently bring your mind back to the practice. In fact, you can count on your mind wandering as you begin these exercises. Bringing your mind back to the practice, over and over again, is also part of the practice and part of training your mind, as you incrementally gain more awareness and focus.

We begin with a fairly simple practice. Set aside five minutes. In this exercise you will want to find a relatively quiet place to sit alone in a chair. After seating yourself comfortably, situate yourself so that your body is fairly upright so that you will be able to breathe freely.

You are about to practice breathing, and giving your full attention to your breathing. Close your eyes so that nothing visually distracts you. Breathe from your belly, from your diaphragm, gently drawing in your breath through your nose and slowly and gently exhaling your breath.

Practicing this exercise, do the following:

Breathe:
From your belly, gently draw in breath through your nose, and gently let the breath out. Don't force it in or out, or try to control your breathing. Just let your breath come in, and let your breath go out. Repeat this for at least three cycles, allowing you time to settle.

Notice:
As you continue breathing, just notice your breath as it enters your nostrils, and as it leaves through your mouth. Notice how it feels entering and exiting gently. Be aware of your breath, giving it your full attention, thinking of nothing else.

Describe:
As you continue breathing, describe your experience of breathing. Say to yourself something like: "I feel my chest expanding and falling," or "My breath is soft," or "I feel my breath leaving my mouth." Let go of judgmental thoughts if they come. Don't entertain thoughts about how strange this is, or that it's weird or a waste of time. Let go of thoughts of any other activities that you can get to later.

When distracting thoughts come, simply describe them: "I notice a thought about laundry just entered my mind," or "This is difficult." Let go of them and come back to your breath.

Engage with Presence:
Stay engaged in this practice. Try to give your full attention to your breath, and only your breath, as it comes in and as it leaves. Acknowledge that it's difficult, if it is, and stay with it for a few minutes.

Stay present with your breathing, giving it your full attention. If you have the urge to quit or to let your mind stray to something you're worried about, turn your focus back toward this moment and your breath, staying with it for just a few minutes. As much as you are able, don't leave this moment, don't check out, leave mentally or daydream. And don't let your mind wander to thoughts about other places you'd rather be, or things you'd rather be doing. Just stay in this one moment.

One Thing: This is the only thing you are doing when you practice. **You are only breathing, and that is all**. You're not thinking about anything else, your full attention is on your breath. Again, let go of distracting thoughts or urges to worry. At this moment, this is all that you are doing. You are training your mind to go where you want it to go, you are increasing your focus. Other activities can wait and will be there for you when you are done with this practice.

ASSESSING YOUR PRACTICE

If this practice was difficult for you, make a brief list of why you think it was difficult.

....
....
....
....

If your mind wandered to other thoughts that distracted you, what were they? List them.

....
....
....
....

If your mind wandered to judgmental thoughts about this practice, what were they?

....
....
....
....

If there were any environmental distractions, what were they (noise outside, temperature, etc)?

....
....
....
....

If you practiced letting go of distractions, list how you noticed and described these distractions, or how you worked at staying present and engaged.

....

....

....

....

When will you commit to yourself to engage in this practice again?

....

....

....

....

✏️ Exercise Two:
AWARENESS OF YOUR ENVIRONMENT

Now that you have a little experience with a specific mindfulness exercise, let's expand your practice a bit. In this exercise you will again want to have a place to sit, setting aside other activities just for a few minutes. In this exercise you will again practice belly breathing, with your eyes closed.

Breathe:

This time, as you close your eyes and begin with three gentle breaths, in through your nose and out through your mouth, and as you settle in and focus on your breath, let your awareness slowly expand to your environment.

Notice:

Allow your awareness to take in all that you experience in your environment as you breathe. Sounds from within the room where you sit, such as the sounds of a ticking clock, the sounds of an air conditioner or heaters, and notice what you experience such as the temperature of the room, the firmness of the chair that holds you.

Notice any smells that come into your nose such as air freshener, dust, incense, whatever is present. Allow your awareness to take in sounds that come in from other rooms or just outside your room, such as the sound of people talking, children playing, wind or traffic — whatever it is that you are aware of through your senses of hearing, smell and touch. Let the sounds, smells or physical feelings just come and go, perhaps lingering a little while on one, and then allow other sensations into your awareness.

Describe:

Describe what you hear, smell or sense with your body again, factually and without judging any of them as good or bad, just the facts. You may say to yourself, "I hear the ticking sound of a clock," or "The sound of children playing has just entered my awareness."

You may say to yourself, "I notice the smell of spring," or "I smell lilacs."

Don't think of these things as distractions; rather let these sensations come and go, not holding onto them for very long, nor pushing them away too quickly.

Engage with Presence:

Staying where you are in your room, sitting in your chair, be present and engaged with this practice, not letting your mind wander to other places. If you notice your attention drifting to other thoughts about anything other than your practice, just notice those thoughts, saying to yourself, "My mind has wandered away from my practice," and then bring yourself back to your practice, turning your attention toward your breath to bring you back to this moment and this practice.

One Thing:

Stay with this practice, not letting anything distract you for these few minutes. At the very moment of your practice, engage in only this practice. Staying with your practice, you are taming your mind and increasing your control over your thoughts.

ASSESSING YOUR PRACTICE

If this practice was difficult for you, make a brief list of why you think it was difficult.

....
....
....

If your mind drifted from your room and the moment you practiced, describe where it went (e.g., worried about bills, thoughts about the past, etc.).

....
....
....

If your mind wandered to judgmental thoughts about this practice, what were they?

....
....
....

If there were any distractions that interfered with your practice, what were they?

....
....
....

If you noticed that you drifted from this practice, describe how you worked at staying present and engaged (e.g., using your breath to come back, etc.).

....
....
....

When will you commit to yourself to engage in this practice again?

....
....
....

STATES OF MIND — BE MINDFUL

WHAT IS MINDFULNESS?

Mindfulness is a state of active, open attention on the present. When you're mindful, you observe your thoughts and feelings from a distance, without judging them as good or bad. Mindfulness means living in the moment and awakening to experience rather than letting your life pass you by.

STATES OF MIND

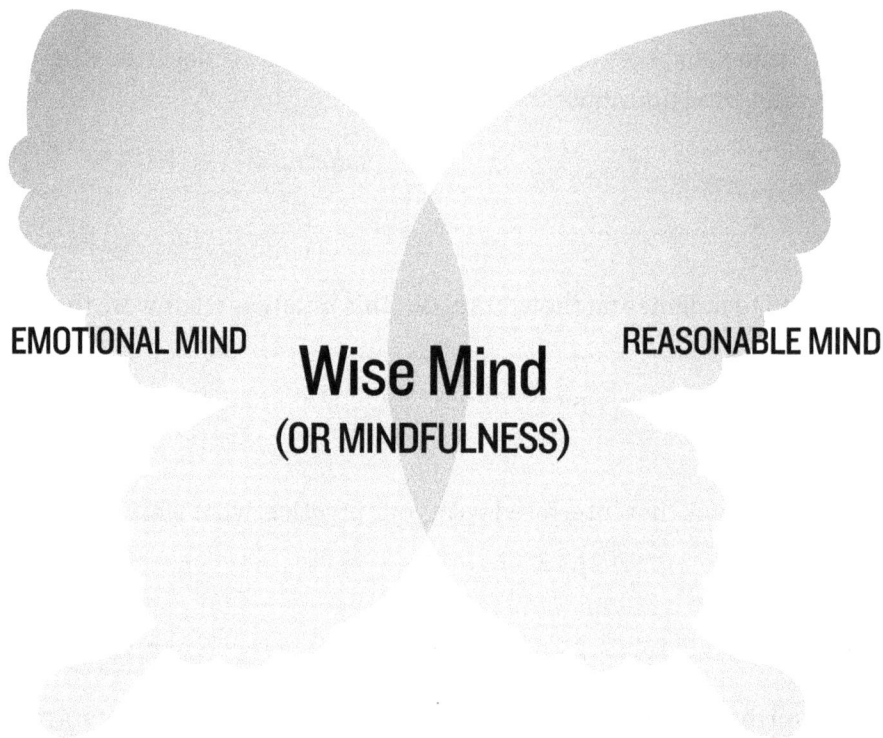

EMOTIONAL MIND   **Wise Mind**   REASONABLE MIND
(OR MINDFULNESS)

EMOTIONAL MIND BEHAVIORS

are controlled by emotions and impulse. Often described as hot and intense. Distorted facts, based on feelings, intense behaviors, high energy, what feels good at the moment.

Examples of Emotional Mind include:

• Arguing with someone over a silly disagreement

• Buying an expensive item on impulse

• Making love

• Taking a walk in the rain because you like it

• Getting mad at your child for spilling a drink

REASONABLE MIND BEHAVIORS

are controlled by logical thinking. Often described as cool and unemotional. Intellectual, logical thinking, planning, attention to facts, focused attention, problem solving.

Examples of Reasonable Mind include:

• Planning all vacation details months ahead

• Bringing a shopping list to the grocery store

• Researching the best price for something on the Internet

• Studying for a test

• Completing a crossword puzzle

Worksheet:

GETTING INTO WISE MIND

TAKE CONTROL OF YOUR MIND

REASONABLE MIND:
- This is your rational, thinking, logical mind
- It plans and evaluates things logically
- It is your "cool" part
- Reasonable Mind can be very beneficial, but when taken to extremes can be very cruel and destructive

EMOTIONAL MIND:
- Emotions can be hot and intense
- Emotions can communicate quickly and influence others
- Emotions are what motivate us to action
- Emotions are what keep us attached to others and building relationships

WISE MIND:
- Wise Mind is the integration of Emotional Mind and Reasonable Mind
- You cannot overcome or control Emotional Mind with Reasonable Mind
- You must go within and integrate these two states of mind
- Peace and connection will result with synthesis of Emotional and Reasonable Mind
- Disconnection and misery will result at the extremes of Emotional Mind and Reasonable Mind

EVERYONE HAS A WISE MIND!
- Some people have simply never experienced it
- No one is in Wise Mind all of the time

the take-away:
Wise Mind integrates the emotional problems with reasonable solutions.

PRACTICING MINDFULNESS

In *You Untangled*, you learned about DBT and the mindfulness skills it teaches. There are the "what" and "how" skills, each broken down to include specific means to increase your awareness in the present moment. This awareness is of your inner self, as well as your environment. The goal is to be aware of, rather than immersed in any one element, of what is going on around you. For example, it is wise and helpful to be aware of your emotions, but it is not useful to be overwhelmed by a particular one. In this section, we will review the DBT "what" and "how" skills, as well as introduce some additional ways to practice mindfulness in your daily life. These practices are designed to increase and strengthen your connection to your true core self. This part of you is your core, untraumatized, pure you. Your essential nature. Our hope is that these skills will appeal to you, and that through this practice of mindfulness, you will reach a level of inner peace and willingness to keep practicing. This is difficult, and that can be a deterrent, but with practice it does get easier.

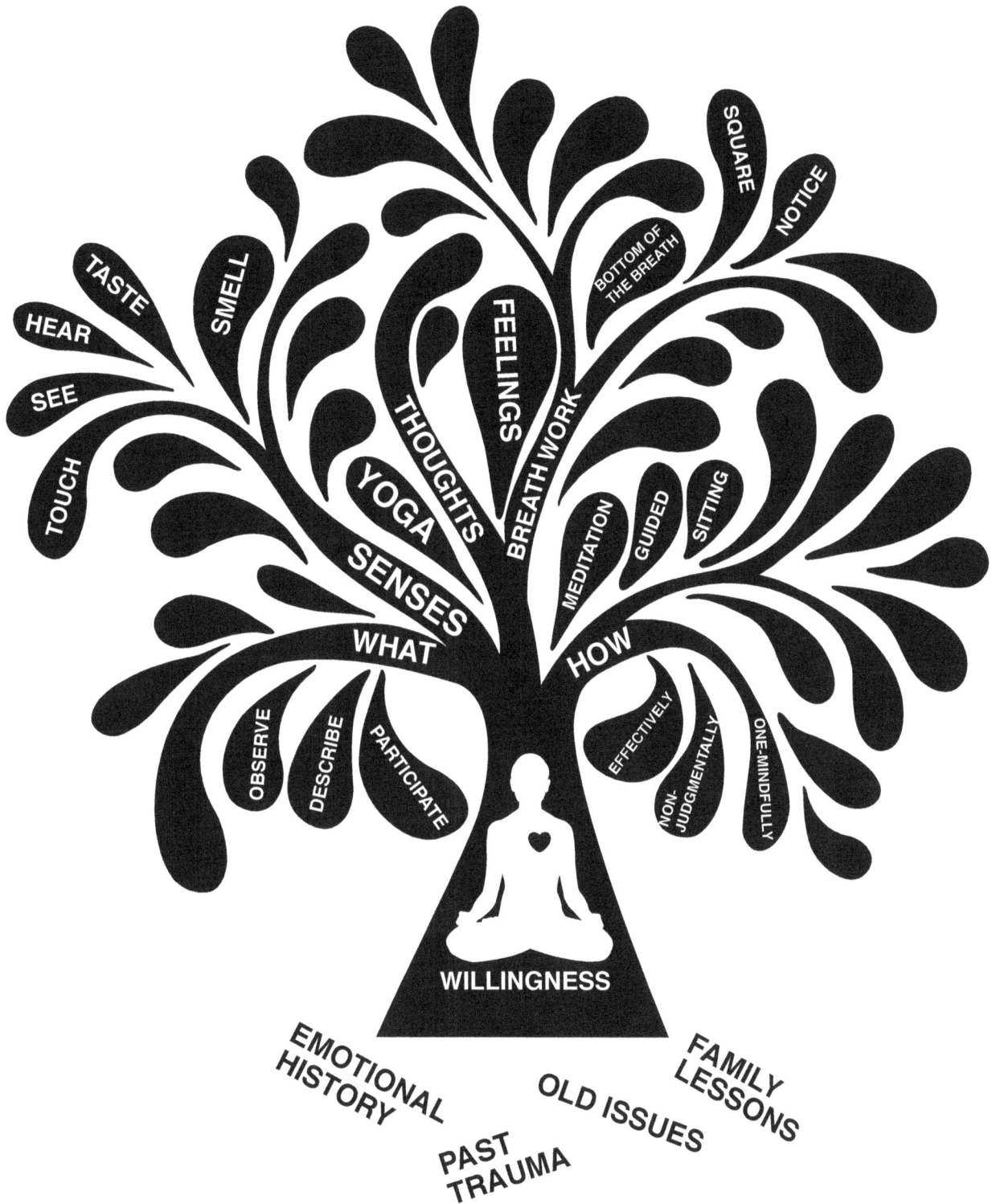

Tree diagram with leaves labeled: SQUARE, NOTICE, BOTTOM OF THE BREATH, FEELINGS, SMELL, TASTE, HEAR, SEE, TOUCH, THOUGHTS, YOGA, BREATH WORK, SENSES, MEDITATION, GUIDED, SITTING, WHAT, HOW, OBSERVE, DESCRIBE, PARTICIPATE, EFFECTIVELY, NON-JUDGMENTALLY, ONE-MINDFULLY. Trunk labeled WILLINGNESS. Roots labeled: EMOTIONAL HISTORY, PAST TRAUMA, OLD ISSUES, FAMILY LESSONS.

With a willingness to practice, you can move beyond all the "root" issues that are holding you back from healthy living.

THE "WHAT" AND "HOW" SKILLS

The "what" and "how" skills are the foundation of mindfulness from a DBT perspective. They are critical to implementing any other skill you have learned, and their usefulness goes beyond being able to utilize the other skills. Before you can process and resolve past trauma, you have to know what you're dealing with, and what the associated emotions are. This is where Observe and Describe are applicable. Additionally, it is a necessary tool to stay present in the moment, with at least one foot firmly planted in the "now." This is where *participating* comes in. **We need to participate in life on life's terms**, and not be overcome by past thoughts, emotions and memories.

The "how" skills enable us to use the skills in a way that works. When we are effective, we are playing by life's rules, and not getting caught up in how things "ought" to be or what is fair or unfair. Being nonjudgmental allows us to let go of a preoccupation with others, or hypervigilance toward ourselves. Noticing what is happening without judgment is incredibly liberating, freeing our energy to be directed toward our goals and living congruently with our values.

Finally, doing things one-mindfully allows us to be in the moment, fully participating in whatever is going on without distraction. These are difficult skills to master but opportunities for practice abound.

As you will see with the additional mindfulness practices that are being presented, there are myriad ways to bring mindfulness into your life. Refer to the end of this chapter for worksheets and excercises on the "what" and "how" skills.

Remember the image of the tree; **through willingness all things are possible**. Be willing to try new things. Be willing to participate in unfamiliar activities in order to find what speaks to you. Allow your branches to grow and reach toward the sky, the sun, the stars.

THE FIVE SENSES

One of the most fundamental things we learn as children is the value of our five senses. When was the last time you intentionally noticed what you smelled? How often do you pay close attention to the taste of your food? Through the five senses: taste, touch, smell, sight and hearing, the world opens to us at a whole new level. Allow yourself to become immersed in the sounds around you, letting the chatter of your mind fade. What do you hear?

....
....
....

Gather some materials to practice attending to the sense of touch. Run your fingers along a piece of sandpaper, noticing its texture. Maybe a sound is also made when you do this. Just notice. You are observing each of your five senses in an effort to be present in the moment, fully attuned to what is going on. You are not clinging or pushing, resisting or hoping. In this moment, you are simply observing what your senses are telling you, without any assessment or judgment. How might you be able to practice being mindful of each of your senses? How will you create an opportunity for practice?

....
....
....

MUNDANE ACTIVITY

Building on the mindfulness practice of noticing your sensory input, now practice being mindful during everyday activities. As you brush your teeth, for example, pay attention to the sound the toothbrush makes on your teeth. Notice the clean smell of the toothpaste. Attend to your hand holding the toothbrush, squeezing the toothpaste, moving the brush over and around all your teeth. How do you breathe while brushing your teeth?

....

....

....

Any activity can be done mindfully. The goal at this point is to begin attending to and noticing your current life without being caught up in thoughts or judgments of the past or others. You can try this while driving, challenging yourself to go slowly or spend time at the stoplight really noticing your surroundings and focusing on your breath. As with all mindfulness, awareness is the goal. Be aware of your body sensations, thoughts and feelings throughout your practice. Remember, you are noticing these without any judgment.

THE PRACTICE OF BREATHING

Focusing on your breath is one of the most fundamental approaches to mindfulness. You can do this at any time, and in lots of different ways. There are practices that involve simply noticing your breath, without any attempt to change it or manipulate it in any way.

Another option is to count your breath, measuring your in-breath and out-breath, adapting it to meet particular needs. If you are aiming to relax, a 4-7-8 count can be helpful. Inhale to the count of 4, through your nose. Hold your breath for a count of 7, then exhale through your mouth for a count of 8, audibly letting your breath go. Complete this cycle three more times. What do you notice?

....

....

....

One particular practice involves finding the space between, or the bottom of the breath. This can be a way to access Wise Mind, or reach a more spiritual awareness. In this exercise, breathe at your regular pace, but place your attention specifically at the space between the inhale and the exhale. Imagine a triangle, and the inhale is the ascent, the exhale is the descent, and the space between is the bottom. Slow your breathing and find this space, without expectation or force, and just notice what happens there.

As you begin to pay attention to your breathing, you may find that it is shallow, or that you hold your breath. Either of these may contribute to an ongoing sense of anxiety or unease. Bringing your attention to your breath, while doing a sitting meditation or as you go about your daily activities, can result in immediate benefits!

How will you focus attention on your breath?

....

....

....

BODY AWARENESS

Mindfulness of the body can be especially challenging for individuals who have experienced trauma. It was likely beneficial to separate yourself from your physical being during past trauma events. This disconnect, while critical during childhood, is likely interfering with your life now. Progressive muscle relaxation and the body scan are two ways that you can reestablish the connection with your body.

Progressive muscle relaxation is a structured activity during which you learn to tense and then relax particular groups of muscles. It was developed by American physician Edmund Jacobson in the early 1920s. You can find many guided scripts for this online.

Body scan can be done in a number of ways. The goal of doing a body scan is to gently place your awareness on different parts of your body, while not judging or trying to make changes. This is an important element to emotion regulation, as you need to be tuned in to yourself in order to be truly in the moment.

Begin by placing your attention on the toes of your right foot. Notice any sensations or thoughts you might have. Remember that there should be no judgment or desire to change anything at this point. You are merely noticing, with curiosity, what is there. Because of the trauma-induced disconnect you may have, this could be a challenging process. Stick with it. Move to the foot as a whole. Stay with each body part for a few moments to a couple minutes, just noticing. As you move through your body, you may find yourself getting distracted, and that's okay. Return and keep going.

As you begin your practice of body awareness, through progressive relaxation or body scan, remember to maintain compassion for yourself and all that your body has been through. Even though things may have occurred far in the past, your body remembers. Be gentle.

TYPES OF MEDITATION

As we've discussed, there are countless ways to practice being mindful. Within this broad scope of mindfulness, we have specific types of meditation. The list below is not all-inclusive; these have been chosen to provide variety and don't require exceptional skills or knowledge. As with all the exercises in this workbook, give each a try, use what works and don't worry about the rest.

Mindfulness meditation, also called "Vipassana," comes from the Buddhist tradition. This is probably the most popular form of meditation in the western world. It's all about "being present." This is the root of the "what" and "how" skills we find in DBT. It is letting your mind run, accepting whatever thoughts come, while also practicing detachment from each thought. Mindfulness is taught along with awareness of breath, though breathing is often considered just one sensation among many others, not of particular focus. You are not attempting to change the breathing pattern, which makes this mindfulness activity one of observation rather than activity.

Take a moment to set a timer, and sit in a comfortable position. Arrange your body so that you will not have to move or shift and can breathe normally. Start in small increments, particularly if you are not at ease sitting still and not "doing" anything. Perhaps three or five minutes will be enough. The timer is an important component because it allows you to fully engage in the practice without having to worry about how long it's been. Just notice your breathing. You are not trying to change anything. Notice what thoughts or feelings arise. You are just observing.

Mantra meditation is another Buddhist tradition. Mantra is a repetition of a word or phrase over and over again. In Buddhism, mantra means "mind protecting." The mind is protected because the mantra prevents it from going into its usual thought pattern. Mantra meditation is a tool that you can use to enter a deep state of meditation. Repetition of the mantra helps you disconnect from thoughts and feelings and possibly even slip into the gaps between. Mantras can be considered ancient power words with subtle intention or traditional prayers of your faith. They can help connect us to spirit, the source of everything in the universe. As you practice this type of meditation, you will experience deeper states where all thoughts and worries gently drop away. This will not come quickly or without commitment and practice. Keep at it and you will find the quiet that always exists beneath the noisy internal chatter of the mind. In this stillness, you may feel oneness with all beings and profound peace.

Choose from the list below or create your own mantra. What do you connect with?

- From the Hindu tradition: Om Namah Shivaya (I bow to Shiva)
- From the Buddhist tradition: Om mani padme hum (I bow to the jewel in the lotus of the heart)
- From the Christian tradition: Hail Mary, full of Grace
- From the Jewish tradition: Shalom (peace)
- From the Muslim tradition: Allahu Akbar (God is great)
- A Sacred Sound mantra: Om (" … In the beginning was the word … and the word was God."). This is also known as the "sound of the universe."
- From the yoga tradition: So Hum ("I am that" – so = "I am" and hum = "that"). Here, "that" refers to all of creation, the one breathing us all.

What practice will you commit to trying?

....

....

....

Put a schedule for yourself below. Include days and times in order to hold yourself accountable to a practice. You will reap immediate benefits from this which will increase significantly over time. You are deserving of the peace and stillness of mind that comes from meditation. Do not lose sight of this, even when it is challenging.

MINDFULNESS "WHAT" SKILLS

OBSERVE

Notice each experience, images, thoughts, sensations, movements and feelings. Both internal and external. Try not to get caught in the experience. Just observe it and let it go. To observe is simply experiencing with awareness of your feelings, thoughts and sensations directly without the use of words. Everything is connected, therefore don't get lost. Stay in the moment. Try to observe every detail of the moment. Try to see both the beauty and the chaos. Don't be a pessimist.

DESCRIBE

Describe is putting words on experience and experience into words. The ability to put verbal labels to (internal and external) events is essential for self-control. Many people rely on the help of a therapist or good friend to describe. It is possible to gain clarity outside awareness through describing in detail your situation to another trusted friend. You can also "describe" by journaling.

PARTICIPATE

Participate is the skill of throwing yourself into your objectives whole-heartedly without self-consciousness. Participate is the "go for it" feeling you have when you enthusiastically pursue an activity meaningful to you. Participate is the satisfying experience of becoming absorbed completely in what you are doing. Your goal is to fully participate in life and enjoy living by letting go of any compulsions or self-defeating behavior.

Adapted from skills Training Manual for Treating Borderline Personality Disorder By Marsha Linehan. ©1993 The Guilford Press

✏ Exercise:
MINDFULNESS "WHAT" SKILLS

Put these skills to practice.

Describe an experience when you were able to use Wise Mind by using the "what" skills. Did using the skill affect your thoughts, feelings or behaviors?

OBSERVE

• Watch your thoughts and feelings and be aware of all connections.
• Do not push away your thoughts and feelings, just let them happen, see fully your reality.
• Focus your full attention on one thing.
• When you fully focus and allow awareness from your senses, you will be able to find clarity in conflict.

....
....
....
....
....
....

DESCRIBE

• Put words on the experience. For example: "I feel sad right now" or "My stomach muscles are tightening" or "I feel sick."

....
....
....
....
....
....

PARTICIPATE

• Become one with your experience: Fully experience your feelings without being self-conscious.

....
....
....
....
....
....

■ Worksheet:
MINDFULNESS "HOW" SKILLS

NON-JUDGMENTALLY

The goal of non-judgmentally is to see things from non-polarized perspectives. Flexibility of thinking is characterized by the ability to entertain other points of view. Consider, too, how you would think about something if you were feeling better. Strive to be factual and separate your opinions from the facts. Try to see things from someone else's point of view. Instead of polarized extremes, activate your Wise Mind to find balance, unity and acceptance.

- Don't evaluate. Just stick to the facts.
- Accept the moment.
- Acknowledge the emotion.

ONE-MINDFULLY

Do one thing at a time. Do not multi-task. It is proven to be much more effective to give your full attention to doing just one thing with all of your focus.

- Concentrate your mind. Do one thing at a time.
- Let go of distractions and give your undivided attention.
- Thinking of one thing at a time decreases anxiety.

EFFECTIVELY

A skill is an ability acquired by training. As you learn and refine skills, you become more effective, i.e., you are able to maximize positive outcomes and minimize negative outcomes. In familiar situations, you know how to maximize benefits because you know from experience what works. But in unfamiliar or difficult situations, when you don't have the benefit of previous experience, you need skills to guide you to the best possible outcome.

- Focus on what works.
- Play by the rules. All of the rules. Do not lie or cheat.
- Keep your eye on what you want in the long run.
- Let go of anger. Anger and vengeance hurts you and doesn't work.

the take-away:

Meet the situation you are in by focusing on what you can control. Practice **radical acceptance** with your mistakes. This will help you learn and grow.

Adapted from skills Training Manual for Treating Borderline Personality Disorder By Marsha Linehan. ©1993 The Guilford Press

✏ Exercise:
MINDFULNESS "HOW" SKILLS

Put these skills to practice.

Describe the experience when you were able to use Wise Mind by using the "how" skills. Did using the skill affect your thoughts feelings or behaviors?

NON-JUDGMENTALLY

....
....
....
....
....
....

ONE-MINDFULLY

....
....
....
....
....
....

EFFECTIVELY

....
....
....
....
....
....

✱ *in* Summary

For more exercises and complete guidelines for how and what to do to get to mindfulness and accessing your internal wisdom, refer to *You Untangled*. Mindfulness skills make up the foundation of the practice of Dialectical Behavior Therapy. DBT skills teach how to bring the skill of mindfulness into everyday practice.

Mindfulness is the cornerstone to mental health. When you master the practice of this skill, you will realize those you know who are not suffering are mindfully present. EMDR can provide the gift of understanding your own mind and how it influences perceptions and actions. When our perceptions are severely limited, we cannot connect to ourselves and the world around us. Mindfulness practice makes it possible to embrace being alive and all the mystery, wonder and glory that can come from truly living in wisdom. EMDR and DBT are therapies that attempt to provide a pathway out of suffering and into living life with wisdom and peace.

Chapter 4

CHAKRA BREATHING & MEDITATION

"Breath is the bridge which connects life to your consciousness, which unites your body to your thoughts. Whenever your mind becomes scattered, use your breath as the means to take hold of your mind again."

Thich Nhat Hanh

In this chapter, you will be introduced to techniques effective in fostering calm and bringing you into the present moment.

HEART CHAKRA MEDITATION

This heart chakra meditation is a simple technique to release sadness and fear and to bring compassion and love into your life.

Sit in a comfortable position, either cross-legged on the floor or in a chair. Sit up tall with the spine straight, the shoulders relaxed and the chest open. Inhale the palms together and lightly press the knuckles of the thumbs into the sternum at the level of your heart (you should feel a little notch where the knuckles magically fit).

Breathe slowly, smoothly and deeply into the belly and into the chest. Soften your gaze or lightly close the eyes. Let go of any thoughts or distractions and let the mind focus on feeling the breath move in and out of your body.

Once the mind feels quiet and still, bring your focus to the light pressure of the thumbs pressing against your chest and feeling the beating of the heart. Keep this focus for one to five minutes.

Next, gently release the hands and rub the palms together, making them very warm and energized. Place the right palm in the center of your chest and the left hand on top of the right. Close your eyes and feel the center of your chest warm and radiant, full of energy. See this energy as an emerald green light, radiating out from the center of your heart into the rest of your body. Feel this energy flowing out into the arms and hands, and flowing back into the heart. Stay with this visualization for one to five minutes.

After you feel completely soaked with heart chakra energy, gently release the palms and turn them outwards with the elbows bent, the shoulders relaxed and the chest open. Feel or visualize the green light love energy flowing out of your palms and into the world. You can direct it toward specific loved ones in your life or to all sentient beings.

To end your meditation, inhale the arms up towards the sky, connecting with the heavens, then exhale and lower the palms lightly to the floor, connecting with the earth. Take a moment or two before moving on with the rest of your day.

CHAKRA BREATHING

- Begin seated. Some people sit on the floor with legs crossed. Others choose a chair. With your eyes closed, breathe consciously, relaxing your muscles.

- In the following pages, you will create a personalized figure to determine where your chakras are. We begin with the site at your **lower spine** (base). Notice where you are seated and feel the connection between the surface where you are seated and your lower spine. To increase your awareness, place the palm of one hand over your lower back/tail bone. With your focus on the lower spine, and while breathing consciously, repeat several times, "I am safe and secure." If you wish, imagine a warm, red glow — the first color of the rainbow — in the lower spine. Continue until you feel ready to move to the next step.

- Bring your awareness to your **lower abdomen** (sacral) by placing a hand on your stomach so that your thumb is on your navel, with the palm of the hand **below the navel**. Repeat, "I am a creative being" as you breathe. Visualize a warm, orange color. Continue until you are ready to move to the next step.

- When you are ready to move on to the third site, move your hand up so your little finger is now on your navel, with the palm of your hand **above the navel** (solar plexus). As you breathe, repeat this phrase: "I can trust my feelings." The color now is yellow: imagine a warm, yellow glow under your hand. Spend a few minutes repeating this.

- Now place your hand over your **heart**, or on your chest, and as you breathe, repeat: "I am worthy of love." Notice how these words are related to your heart. The color is now green. You are not trying to indoctrinate yourself with words, but simply bringing your attention to what you are saying. Repeat until you feel ready to move on. Continue as long as you wish.

- Place your hand now on your **throat**, and breathe with the words, "I can tell the truth." Notice again the relevance of the words for your throat, which is so important for expressing ourselves. The color here is blue.

- Bring your awareness to your **forehead** and place your hand there. Imagine the next color of the rainbow, a little ball of indigo that spreads slowly to the rest of your head, from your eyebrows down. The words to repeat along with your breathing are these: "I can see things clearly."

- Finally, place your hand on **top of your head** (crown) and imagine a ball of the last rainbow color, violet. The words now are, "I am transcendent." Repeat these words for several minutes or until you feel ready to stop this exercise.

- Use the breathing exercise until you are comfortable with the chakras. When you feel connected to this, use the next page to visually represent your experience.

✎ Exercise:

COLOR YOUR HEART CHAKRA

From what you learned in the last section, color your heart chakra!

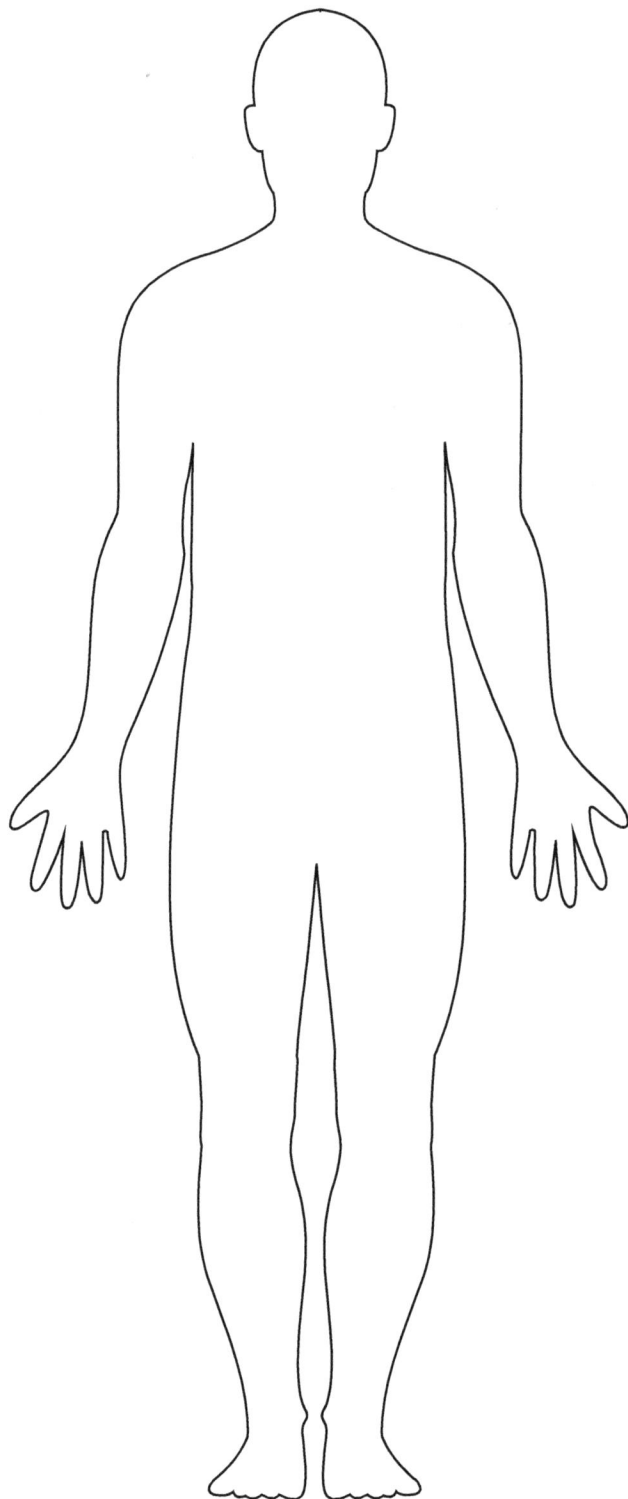

Worksheet:

SELF-SOOTHING WITH A BUTTERFLY HUG

First introduced by Lucy Artigas in 1997 while she was working with hurricane survivors in Mexico, the butterfly hug is an EMDR technique designed to be used by an individual as a self-soothing technique to reduce anxiety and strengthen positive sensations.

Sit comfortably and place your hands on your shoulders so that your arms are crossed. As you notice an unpleasant memory, gently tap your shoulders in an alternating pattern at whatever speed you feel comfortable, although it should not be too fast. Continue tapping until you notice that the distress in decreasing. It is helpful to begin the exercise by rating your distress so that you can determine how much it has gone down.

Another way to utilize the butterfly hug is to increase positive sensations. Begin by remembering a time in which you felt competent, loved, safe or important. As you hold this memory, along with all the physical and emotional sensations it brings, tap your shoulders. Notice the positive sensations increasing as you tap, and continue as long as you feel it is helpful.

Chapter 5

STRESS REDUCTION & SLEEP HYGIENE

"Even a soul submerged in sleep is hard at work and helps make something of the world."

Heraclitus

In this chapter, we are addressing the physical aspects of managing stress and increasing mindfulness. It is important to pay attention to what might contribute to your distress in the here and now. It is equally important to determine how you can minimize that distress.

Worksheet:
STRESS LESS — 4 ELEMENTS

Stress reduction is paramount to reducing chaos and instability in your life. We all have daily stressors in the form of work, life and family demands, but keeping stress in check is critical to overall well-being. Here are some tips and exercises to help you achieve a lower level of stress in your life. Begin at the bottom, and work your way up.

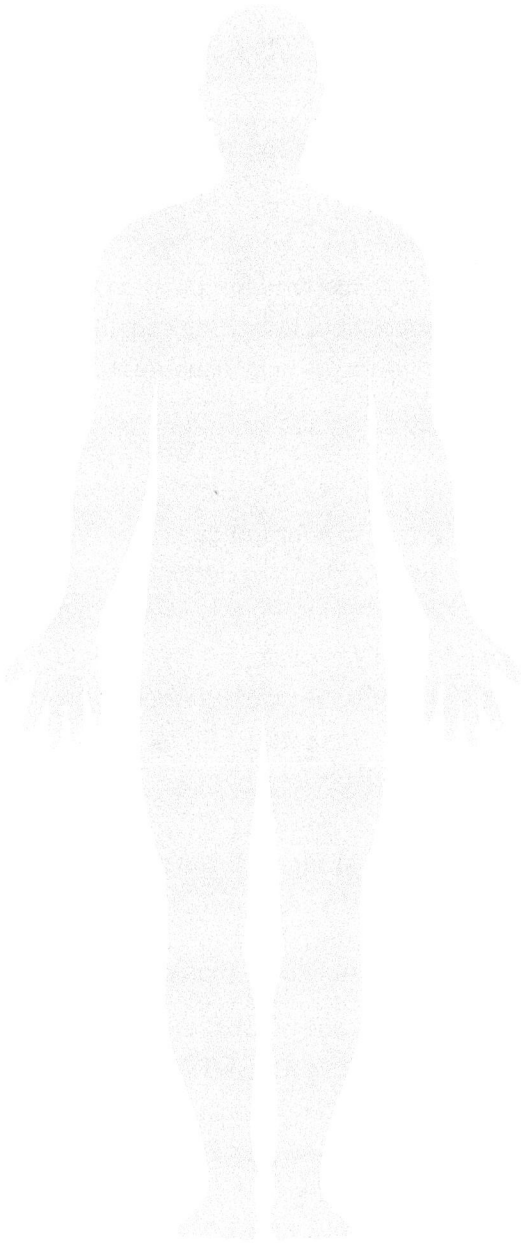

Fire: **Light Up The Path Of Your Imagination.** Bring up the image of your *safe place* or some other positive resource. Where do you feel it in your body?

Water: **Calm And Controlled To Switch On The Relaxation Response.** Check to see if you have saliva in your mouth. Make more saliva by moving your tongue around and imagining the taste of a lemon (or chocolate). When you are anxious or stressed, your mouth often "dries" because part of the stress emergency response involved in "fight or flight" shuts off the digestive system. So it seems that when you start making saliva, you switch on the digestive system again and the associated relaxation response. If you have difficulty making saliva, then start yourself off with a sip of water.

Air: **Breathing For Centering.** You can use your favorite breathing exercise here. Another option is to breathe in through your nose as you count four seconds, then hold it for two, then breathe out for four seconds. Take about a dozen deep, slow breaths like this.

Earth: **Grounding, Safety In The Present/ Reality.** Take a minute or two to "land" and to be here now. Place both feet on the ground and feel the chair supporting you. Look around and notice three new things. What do you see? What do you hear?

Adapted from "Getting Past Your Past" by Francine Shapiro, Ph.D.

✏ Exercise:
ACTIVATING THE GOOD STUFF

This exercise is designed to activate the part of your nervous system that is responsible for creating positive feeling, as well as reducing stress. In the earlier section on trauma, we talked about "fight or flight." That is your sympathetic nervous system in action.

We want to learn how to intentionally activate your "rest and digest," or parasympathetic, nervous system. This is the part of you designed to relax you once a threat has passed, and the part that may not have gotten enough opportunity to work.

If you have experienced multiple traumas in your life, or grew up in a particularly chaotic and stressful environment, then your sympathetic nervous system has likely been over-stimulated. If so, you may find it difficult to relax. Below are some exercises that can help activate your parasympathetic system (PNS) and soothe your sympathetic system.

Begin by rating your distress or discomfort from zero to 10, where 10 is the most intense upset.

Exercise #1: Take deep breaths. When inhaling, completely fill the lungs, hold for a second, and then exhale slowly. Try doing this for a whole minute. This relaxed method of breathing expands the branches in your airways called bronchioles, activating the PNS that controls them, causing them (and the rest of the body and mind) to relax.

Exercise #2: Relax your body. Try basic stretching or a breathing meditation. You can simply close your eyes and visualize a comfortable place, somewhere familiar or in your imagination. The parasympathetic nervous system causes you to relax, but by "actively" relaxing, you activate it, causing you to relax even more. Call it a non-vicious circle.

After you have completed one or both exercises, return to the rating of your distress.

Has it decreased in intensity? Keep practicing until you can successfully decrease your upset.

Sometimes our body becomes tense and stressed because of negative thoughts. If this is the case, it may work to change your thinking, something you have undoubtedly tried.

However, that is not always possible.

In those situations, remember that you can change your body to elicit a similar calming response. This is called a "bottom-up" solution, versus "top-down," where the goal is to change your experience by changing your mind.

Exercise #3: Breathe so that your inhalation and exhalation last the same amount of time; for example, you might count slowly to five for each.

While doing this, imagine this breath coming in and out of your heart center in your chest, radiating love, gratitude and peace. Integrate this positive emotion into your own brain. This exercise is called "increasing heart rate variability"; it increases and harmonizes the variation in heart beats, activating the PNS to enhance physical and mental well-being.

SLEEP HYGIENE JOURNAL

Use this chart to track your progress. Note what time you are doing each activity, and notice any patterns that may be contributing to your troubled sleep.

Day/Time	Routine/Ritual	Caffeine/Meds	Exercise	Notes
Monday				
Tuesday				
Wednesday				
Thursday				
Friday				
Saturday				
Sunday				

Chapter 6

TRAUMA EFFECT AND RESPONSES

"We often get caught up in our own reactions and forget the vulnerability of the person in front of us."

Sharon Salzberg

In this chapter, you will learn techniques to take in positive experiences. Learning how to take in the good, no matter the darkness around you, will lead to resilience. Resilience is key to thriving. If you are thriving, you can find a way to appreciate life and build a fulfilling future.

HOW TO TAKE IN A POSITIVE EXPERIENCE

As we've seen, memories and past experiences significantly influence our lives. Trauma interferes with our ability to take in a positive experience. We are where we've been, and what we've experienced. There are two kinds of memories: explicit and implicit. This gets slightly technical, but hang in there; it's worth it!

Explicit memory: Recollections of specific events.
Implicit memory: Emotions, body sensations, relationships and our sense of the world.

Implicit memory is the memory that stirs your "gut feelings." It is the felt sense you have, and is an ancient part of your brain structure (think amygdala and limbic system).

This is an important distinction to make, as our sense of self and what it feels like to be *you* is rooted in your emotional memories. Therefore, it is of utmost importance to be mindful and take care of what is held in your implicit memory.

Why bother?

Negative experiences are registered immediately. This is an evolutionary remnant because we once had to keep track of danger in order to survive. In order for positive experiences to register in our memory, it has to be attended to and held for five to 20 seconds.

Negative experiences also trump positive ones; for example, one bad experience with a dog is more memorable than 100 good ones. We have to deliberately register positive experiences so that they settle into the deepest layers of our brain.

By taking in positive experiences, you are creating the foundation for self-soothing (distress tolerance!), emotional self-regulation and resilience. This will make your life easier. This is also a crucial internal resource and path for healing from trauma. You are choosing to attend to reality, and not just wearing rose-tinted glasses. Use new positive experiences to counter the old, negative ones.

HOW TO DO IT!

Now that you're ready to try this, how is it done?

Focus on the emotional and bodily sensations associated with your positive experiences. You may use the butterfly hug to reinforce these sensations as you hold the experience and create implicit positive memories.

Be in reality. You are being fair and seeing the truth. Don't judge or cherry-pick, and challenge yourself to use your newly-honed insight.

Recognize the importance of practicing taking in the good. If you integrate positive experiences, you are building confidence and faith in the path of life, and are more able to care for and be kind to others.

Be aware of pitfalls. There will be people who say it is a bad or selfish thing to feel good, especially about yourself. Those voices may even come from inside you. Explore those attitudes, and then gently let them go by relaxing your body, releasing the associated emotions, and challenging the illogical beliefs of this attitude.

✏ Exercise:

now, you do it:
TAKE IN A POSITIVE EXPERIENCE

List positive experiences that you would like to more strongly integrate into your implicit memory.

....

....

....

....

What are the facts of the situation? What emotions and body sensations were created when you reflect on this event or experience?

....

....

....

....

If you struggle to come up with a personal experience, what might be a more general event that you can use to begin this practice? Pay attention to what is in your environment: a pretty sunset, a good song on the radio, completing a task, going to the gym, the smell of a baby.

....

....

....

....

Maintain a relaxed and accepting posture during this exercise. Set aside concerns or irritations. Keep your attention on this experience for an extended length of time, at least 20-30 seconds. Don't jump to something else; remember, it takes that long for the memory to be embedded in your brain. Let it fill your body with positive sensations and emotions, going down into the old wounds and replacing them with new and pleasant experiences. Reflect on your experience with this exercise below.

....

....

....

....

Often, the most valuable memories to loosen and replace are those painful ones from childhood. These are the roots of our pain and difficulty in life.

We must pull the entire weed in order to keep it from growing back time and again. The best way to do this is to hold at the same time the new and positive experience and the old painful one.

Let the positive be in the foreground, and the past be in the background. Allow it to dim and fade until it is replaced by new experiences, sensing your body and emotions as you practice this exercise. You aren't forgetting old things, but the emotional charge will be gone. These exercises change your brain!

Additional places to look for resources and positive experiences.

Look for opportunities to feel these in the moment, and reflect on the past for occurrences, as well.

Feeling safe and secure, protected and with someone accepting.

....
....
....
....

Experiencing gratitude and appreciation, even for the smallest thing.

....
....
....
....

Strength and resilience. Any time you were determined or used your will and assertiveness.

....
....
....
....

Feeling loved and cared about, liked.

....
....
....
....

An experience of feeling value and competency, capable and "good enough."

....
....
....
....

Look inside yourself. **Who are you at your best?** What sort of person are you when you're not threatened or stressed? This innate goodness and fundamental nature is pure and peaceful, kind and wise. Tune into this.

....

....

....

....

Chapter 7

GAINING INSIGHT

"We either make ourselves miserable or we make ourselves strong. The amount of work is the same."

Carlos Castenada

In this chapter, you will learn to make sense of your world and recognize your purpose in life. The answers are within us and we simply have to understand ourselves better to see how to overcome the barriers. You will learn to be an observer and then direct your own life.

WHAT IS INSIGHT?

Insight means being able to look within, and be an observer. You are able to separate your past from your present, and use what is useful while leaving the rest. Your actions and reactions are not fixed, and as you gain insight you can see how internal factors have influenced your current functioning and how to change them.

SEEING WHAT IS

In order to gain and increase insight, you have to allow yourself to see the truth. You must want to see the truth, even if it is painful or uncomfortable. What is your truth? What might you be resisting or avoiding that prevents insight?

....

....

....

....

UNIVERSAL CAUSES

There is a cause for everything. Some of these causes may be set at birth, including temperament and gender, or early in life, as in our attachment style. Other causes are race, class, religion or culture. Whatever the cause for where you are in life, it is beneficial to explore these factors in order to gain insight and make mindful choices and changes.

TEMPERAMENT

Temperament is defined by the mostly stable and unchanging characteristics of you. These are naturally set at birth, and need to be learned to be managed skillfully.

How would you define your temperament? Are you an observer? Do you sit back and take it in before deciding how to proceed? Do you tend to describe? Are you the person who chats with everyone, wanting to talk and make sense of things that way? Do you participate? Do you jump into activities and events, willing to get involved with whatever comes your way?

Take a moment and reflect on what your temperament is. What is your default emotion? How does this influence your ability to gain and maintain insight? What adaptations need to be made to skillfully adjust to and manage your personal style?

....

....

....

....

ORIENTATION TO THE WORLD

How do you relate to people in the world? Do you move toward them, away from them, or against them? Know that if you challenge your typical orientation, things can still be OK.

What kind of experiences can you create in order to deliberately go against your inclination?

Take that experience and make it a part of you. It is evidence that change is OK.

....

....

....

....

GENDER

Two tasks of our development are becoming independent of our family and getting close to those we choose. We seek to be individuals, independent and unique. We also seek connection, and to be part of the whole.

How has gender impacted your independence? How does it affect how you get close to people? How is gender viewed in your family? Are there specific roles? What does it look like when your independence or intimacy is threatened? How does the push and pull of relationships work?

Think dialectically, remembering that neither is right or wrong.

Are there perceived threats that may not really be there? What is the priority for other people in your life? Knowing these things can help you be more effective interpersonally.

....

....

....

....

ATTACHMENT & DISTANCE

We all have an attachment style, and knowing what yours is can help you navigate relationships more effectively.

Attachment begins before birth, and is a critical part of how we function in life. Our earliest learning occurs in the relationship we have with our primary caregiver. This is usually, but not always, the mother. We learn lessons about how the world works and our place in it from that relationship. Exploring that, and how it may translate to your current life, can be a gratifying — yet sometimes painful — process.

Was your mom (you can imagine whomever your primary caregiver was; for simplicity, I will refer mostly to mothers) nurturing and responsive? Was a distinction made between *you* as a person and your behavior? More specifically, were you valued and loved no matter what, or was it based on your actions? If you were raised in an environment where affection was conditional, you may use harmful behavior now to get close to people.

What is your distance preference? Do you seek attention and admiration or compliments from others? Does that provide you energy and satisfaction? Or, are you more comfortable keeping your distance, and not very comfortable getting close to others? Do you feel invaded by people getting close and depleted by emotional connection?

Ways to increase your insight, if you tend to keep distance, include being aware of your fears and practicing letting them go, experiencing that it is OK to be close.

Remind yourself that you are well protected and can handle relating to others.

If you tend to seek attention, don't shame yourself for it; rather, address these drives as an opportunity to build resources and fill your empty spaces. Accomplish and be productive in an authentic way, and beware the urge to have expectations based on your "supposed-tos."

Be aware of extreme experiences, either positive or negative, and view them as experiences like any other. Let go of them and internalize healthy alternatives.

Use the space below to reflect on how your attachment and distance styles have impacted your view of yourself and your experience in relationships.

....
....
....
....

RACE/CLASS

How do you identify in terms of race and class? How have these characteristics informed your experiences and shaped your view of yourself? Are there qualities you've adopted because they fit with your race or class but may not be true to yourself?

Be mindful of these subtleties, and identify what works and what doesn't for the goals and values you have chosen for yourself.

....
....
....
....

RELIGION & CULTURE

What role does your religion and culture play in your life? How has your religious upbringing impacted your view of yourself? Is it in line with who you want to be?

This is another factor that can influence your ability to have insight, and the challenge is to address mindfully those elements that work and those that don't.

How has your culture shaped your self-view? Do you mindlessly go along with things because "that's just how it's done?" Examine the impact of these significant factors in order to increase insight.

....
....
....
....

CAUSING CHANGE

Once you have spent time reflecting on and examining the myriad factors that influence our view of self, work on determining what you would like to keep and what no longer works.

....
....
....
....

What are the great legacies of your:

Gender

....
....
....

Attachment

....
....
....

Culture

....
....
....

Religion

....
....
....

What would be better left in the past?

....
....
....

To further this experience, bring up a slightly distressing recent event. On a scale of 1-10, choose something that is around a 2 or 3 in terms of intensity. Using mindfulness and insight, you will practice letting it go.

First, review the facts of the event. Describe these non-judgmentally.

....

....

....

What are the reactions it stirs inside you? Scan your body from top to bottom and notice any distress, tension, or disturbance.

....

....

....

Reflect on how you are acting in the present as a result of this reflection. How do the thoughts and body sensations impact you?

....

....

....

Now, try to sense what part of your response is based on a younger you. What feelings may be linked to something similar from childhood? As you move through this exercise, you might want to use the butterfly hug to help this information move.

....

....

....

What might your wants or needs from childhood be that are being tapped into now?

....

....

....

How has your childhood perspective gotten twisted up into your adult view? Do you notice yourself responding in ways that are more childlike than adult? What could be the strategies or styles from childhood that are occurring these days?

....

....

....

Chapter 8

FAMILY SYSTEMS

"If you cannot get rid of the family skeleton, you may as well make it dance."

George Bernard Shaw

In this chapter, you will begin to understand the generational dilemmas that have been passed down. Oftentimes we carry challenges, shame or struggle that is not our burden to bear. Our love and connection to our families leave us wanting to address their problems and pain. We are driven to save ourselves and our families.

GENOGRAMS AND FAMILY SYSTEMS

Many therapies use the genogram to get a big picture of a family system.

It is basically a family tree, using particular lines and symbols to represent certain things. This can be especially helpful in families where abuse or neglect is passed from generation to generation.

A genogram is simply another way of assessing and viewing your risk factors for PTSD and Complex PTSD. It is also useful to see where relationships are healthy, enmeshed or dysfunctional. By using the specific lines and shapes, you can see the trends and habits that are present in your family system.

Although this may look complicated, you aren't bound to use all these symbols. Do what works for you, and make it useful.

Example Family Genogram

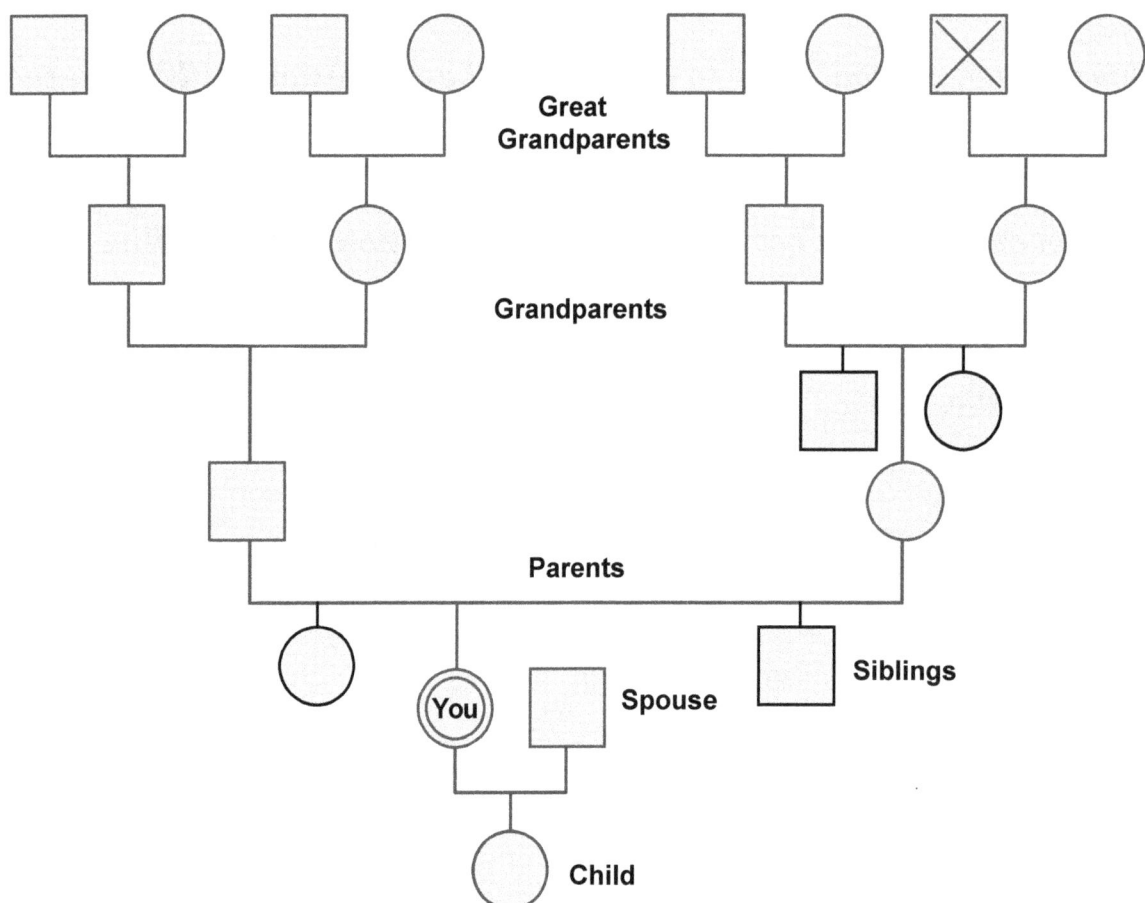

✏ Exercise:

now, you do it:
CREATE YOU FAMILY GENOGRAM

Once you have people mapped out, use the different line styles to connect individuals (close, distant, abusive). Shade the lower half of the shape if the person has substance abuse issues and the right half if there are mental health issues. (Note divorce, cause of death, conflict or distance in order to more fully understand the legacy of your family.)

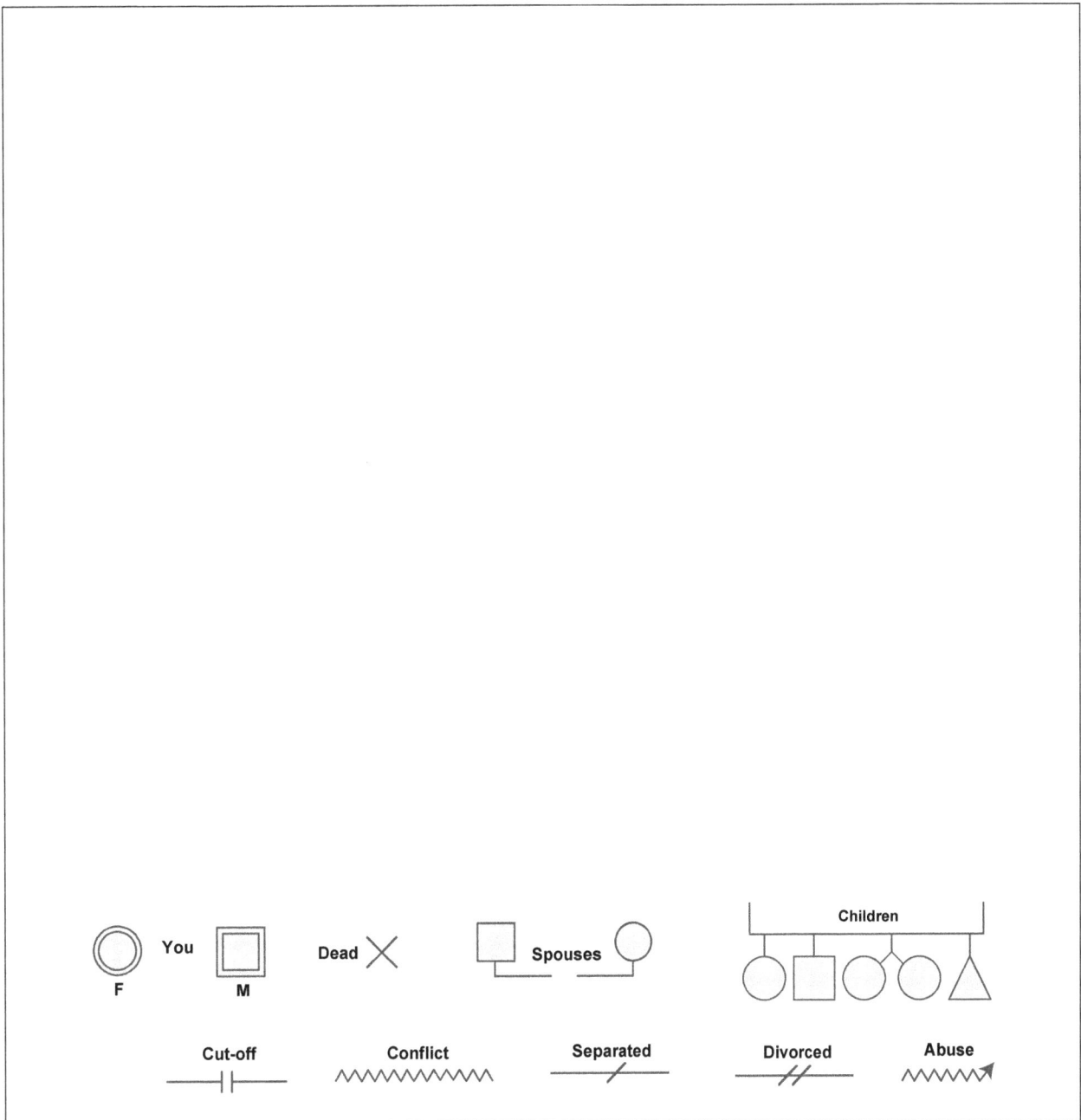

○ You ☐ M Dead ✕ ☐ Spouses ○ Children ○☐○○△

Cut-off ─┤├─ Conflict ∧∧∧∧∧∧ Separated ──/── Divorced ──//── Abuse ∧∧∧∧➔

What relationship patterns do you notice?

....

....

....

....

Are there generational patterns?

....

....

....

....

Are there people who are close and some who are distant?

....

....

....

....

As you explore what patterns may exist in your family tree, it might be helpful to look at the generations before yours. What are the legacies that your parents have brought with them into their own parenting style? How did they learn to experience and express emotion and how did they pass that down to you? It is not uncommon for individuals to want to parent in a way completely opposite of how they were parented. If you have children, how does your parenting impact how you choose to parent?

Using the genogram can provide valuable insight to how individual family members interact and function. Are there characteristics that could be made sense of based on birth order? How does being the oldest of many siblings perhaps look different than the experience of an only child? Were you raised by your birth parents? If someone else raised you, how does that shape your view of yourself and your place in the world?

Consider your place in the family tree. Are you close to siblings or cousins that are similar in age? Why or why not? Are you distant from people whom you'd like to be closer to? How do the connections, or lack of connections, influence you in day-to-day functioning? What might you benefit from if you were to reconnect with those who are distant?

Being separate from your family of origin may be a healthy choice for you. However, it is also common for individuals to isolate themselves in order to feel safer, only to find they are lonely and depressed as a result.

Is there a change for you to make with a family member in order to continue on your path of reconnection and transformation? Can you make a commitment now, to yourself, to make that change?

Chapter 9

MEMORIES, BELIEFS & LIFE STAGES

"Sometimes you will never know the value of a moment until it becomes a memory."

Dr. Seuss

In the following pages, you will become familiar with the eight life stages.

You will learn why struggling and failing to thrive through these stages has a

long-lasting impact on your health and well-being. We will also practice ways

to complete unmastered developmental tasks. Trauma prevents you from moving

smoothly through life stages. It's possible you may be stuck in one stage or

another. Remember to be gentle on yourself and take your time.

EIGHT LIFE STAGES

Erik Erikson was a developmental psychologist who identified eight life phases, each with its own "task" to be faced.

Depending on how these were experienced, you may have gotten stuck in one phase or another. This section will help you explore each phase and what may have helped or hindered your mastery of each task.

There will be a lot of ground to cover, so this chapter has been divided up into sub-segments. Take your time on this, seeking help where you need it in order to thoroughly and mindfully look at each stage.

The goal of our development is not to avoid struggle. The most skilled parents do not prevent their child from experiencing difficulty. Rather, they provide support and validation, as well as a safe place to experience life. They will intervene when necessary, if the child is in danger or extremely frustrated, but the goal is also to allow the child to experience mastery and a sense of comfort and competence in their environment.

To help provide a context for your childhood and how it may be impacting your adult life, consider the ACES study, which was conducted at Kaiser Permanente from 1995-1997 by the Centers for Disease Control and Prevention (CDC).

The goal of the study was to examine what early childhood experiences impacted health later in life. In fact, 17,000 participants were enrolled and have since been tracked and their health monitored. ACE stands for "adverse childhood experiences" and includes three main categories: abuse, neglect and dysfunction. The more ACEs you have prior to age 18, the more likely you are to experience an increase in health problems in these areas:

- Alcoholism and alcohol abuse
- Chronic obstructive pulmonary disease (COPD)
- Depression
- Fetal death
- Health-related decrease in quality of life
- Illicit drug use
- Ischemic heart disease (IHD)
- Liver disease
- Risk for intimate partner violence
- Multiple sexual partners
- Sexually transmitted diseases (STDs)
- Smoking
- Suicide attempts
- Unintended pregnancies
- Early initiation of smoking
- Early initiation of sexual activity
- Adolescent pregnancy

This is the science behind the issues that you may be facing. This is not to make you feel hopeless or doomed. Nor is it to point fingers or assign blame to something that is in the past.

However, if you have questioned why or how you've ended up in your current situation, perhaps this will shed some much needed light on things. It can help you identify and separate what may be an influence from past experiences and how to stay present with the things over which you have control now.

Are any of the above listed problems things you've experienced?

....

....

....

....

As you work through each developmental stage, take time to reflect on how those experiences could have led to health problems.

Pay special attention to your bodily reactions to thinking about this now, and what emotions come up.

There are visualization exercises to try as you work through the developmental stages of your past.

The exercises rely, in part, on the fact that the area of your brain in which trauma is stored is not concerned with accurate time and space.

Your unconscious mind is also not particularly concerned with facts or reality.

Both of these facts allow visualization to work; you can come and go through past events, reshaping and emphasizing different elements in order to store them adaptively.

Every time an event is recalled, it changes slightly (this is why eye witness reports are notoriously unreliable). Because these shifts already occur, we can utilize them for our own purposes, revisiting and re-experiencing events in order to resolve them. These can create strong emotional responses.

It is important that you have already spent time on relaxation and mindfulness exercises so that you can refer back to them as needed.

If an exercise becomes too intense, it is always OK to stop. Ground yourself and continue the process when you are ready.

Before you begin the visualizations, rate your distress around the memory and in the current moment on a scale of 0 to 10, with 10 being the most upsetting. After you're done, rank it again to determine if you've achieved some relief.

No matter what part of the book you're in, it is also important to make sure you have limited your vulnerability factors. Be sure that you have eaten and are rested. Do not try this work if you are upset about another situation or struggling with a current crisis.

Although it may seem there is never a "good time" for trauma work, you want to make sure you are taking care of yourself to avoid any further traumatization. Consult a therapist as needed.

Good luck on your journey and be gentle with yourself.

PART I: INFANCY & EARLY CHILDHOOD

"Childhood lasts all through life."

Gaston Bachelard

In this section, you will explore the beginning of your life and perhaps find the root of some of your negative thoughts. Resolving and healing trauma from infancy can be tricky due to the foundation of your memories being formed during this time. Be compassionate with yourself.

BIRTH TO 1 — INFANT

From birth to age 1, the task to master was whether to trust or mistrust. The most important relationship at this time is the one with your mother. For infants who establish trust, they have faith in the environment and their future. Trust is built when the primary caregiver predictably provides food, warmth and comfort. If the baby cried, Mom would come. The big question is, "Can I trust the world?"

If these most basic needs are not met, an infant might be suspicious or fearful. If your infant needs were not met, you likely have difficulty trusting people. If you can't trust your parents to love and care for you, how could you trust anyone else? This is the identity crisis faced by many individuals struggling with BPD.

Use the space below to identify any memories or information you have from your very first year. If possible, talk to those who knew you at that time if you don't know much.

What was your living arrangement?

....
....
....
....

Who were the major people in your life?

....
....
....
....

Were there any factors that may have complicated your development?

....
....
....
....

After you have reflected on this stage of your life, can you identify examples in which you developed mistrust in someone or your environment? Perhaps your parent used alcohol or drugs and was not attentive to your basic needs?

....
....
....
....

Now, direct your focus toward situations in which you were able to trust. Was there a babysitter or grandparent who cared for you? When were those basic needs met?

....

....

....

....

What is the answer to that initial question? Can you trust the world?

....

....

....

....

Oftentimes, we develop ideas about ourselves and the world based on these early experiences. This is where trauma can begin, and get rooted. Based on the examples above, what did you learn about yourself and the world? What do you believe about yourself as a result of these experiences?

....

....

....

....

What do you believe about the world?

....

....

....

....

What conclusion do you come to in general? This can often show up in "negative cognitions," or thoughts. These are the beliefs that EMDR works to dislodge, and usually fall into the categories of worth, safety or responsibility. For example: "I'm unlovable," "I'm bad" or "It's all my fault."

Can you identify a negative thought about yourself that results from not developing trust?

Now, go back to some of your positive memories from above, situations in which you were able to establish trust. What belief about yourself developed from that? For instance, it may be "I'm OK," "I'm loved" or "I did the best I could."

The process of resolving and healing trauma requires you to choose.

Which belief are you going to maintain, the positive or negative?

Can you come up with some statements to challenge the negative thought? Remember that while most trauma memory is stored in the sensory/emotion part of the brain, you have developed thoughts and beliefs about it, as well. What flaws are there to your logic? If you were not yet 1 year old, how much responsibility or blame could you *really* have?

✏️ Exercise:
VISUALIZATION — INFANT

Get into a relaxed position, lying down or sitting in a comfortable chair. Begin by taking three long, slow, deep breaths. As you do, notice your body sinking down into your seat, tension releasing from your shoulders, legs and core.

As you relax, picture a landscape of your life. Imagine all the details of the landscape, from the trees to the sky, and any other elements that may be present. It could be a park or forest, a beach or mountain.

In this landscape, imagine a path. As you travel on this path, you move back in time throughout your life. There are memories and images from all phases of your life.

Go to the beginning of the path, and imagine the home you lived in as an infant. Pull up a picture of the house, apartment or trailer you lived in, and the room inside where you slept. If you don't know what your home looked like, make up anything that feels right. Spend some time imagining all the details that you can in order to create a vivid image.

As you move into your home, make your way to the bedroom. Where did you sleep? Can you see your tiny baby self in the crib or bed? Study your fingers and nose, the peaceful sleep of your infant self.

As you watch, imagine the baby wakes and begins to cry. Your mom or caregiver enters and attempts to address your needs. However, she is unable to tend to you successfully. She tries to feed you, not realizing your diaper is wet. Watch as you continue to fuss and cry, and your caretaker leaves the room.

Now, you start crying again, and this time your adult self comes into the room. Pick up the baby. Rock and cuddle, kissing your infant self on the forehead. Offer a bottle, and hold the baby close. Talk to your infant self as you begin to settle. You calm the baby, and say to her (or him):

I love you.
I am so glad you're here.
Welcome, you are special and unique.
I'll never leave you.
Whatever else you'd like to add, share with your baby self.

Now switch perspectives. Instead of being an invisible bystander, imagine yourself as the infant when your parent comes in and is unable to meet your needs. Create a vivid image just as before, with all the sights, sounds and smells you can picture. Feel yourself calm as your adult self comes in to comfort you.

Take as much time with this visualization as you need. When you are finished, breathe deeply and return with intention to the present moment. This visualization can be especially helpful when the negative beliefs listed above come forward and are overwhelming. If you feel helpless or insecure, this visualization can be beneficial.

1-3 TODDLERHOOD

The task to master at this stage of development is referred to as "autonomy versus doubt." This comes down to how you view yourself, either confidently or with doubt. As you grow, during this time, your job is to learn to dress yourself and use the toilet. The most important people in your life are your parents, who support your growing self-will.

A child who navigates this time in a caring and nurturing environment grows to have a sense of adequacy and self-control. If you were in such an environment, you probably feel generally OK about yourself and your ability to move about the world.

If you were in a hostile or inattentive environment, though, you may have developed a general sense of shame and doubt. You might not have confidence about your worth. Was potty training a shameful experience? Were you supported in making your own choices, or were your parents critical or controlling? If this was the case, you may feel unable to make decisions and feel overly dependent on others.

What are your memories of this time? Were both of your parents present?

....
....
....
....

Were you encouraged to explore your surroundings and make choices about what you wore or played with?

....
....
....
....

Do you know much about your potty training experience? How did it go?

....
....
....
....

Everyone has experienced both negative and positive events at all life stages. Identify three examples in which you felt stifled or controlled, most likely by your parents, during toddler years. As before, consult people who may be able to provide information that you might not remember.

....
....
....
....

No matter what your childhood circumstances, there are examples of independence and doubt for everyone.

List three examples in which you were encouraged to explore and make your own choices.

....

....

....

....

The existential question that toddlers face is whether or not it is OK to be themselves. How do you answer that question?

....

....

....

....

What are your beliefs about yourself, learned from this young age?

....

....

....

....

What do you believe about the world as a result? Is your experience that you can be yourself and feel accepted by people?

....

....

....

....

If not, how do you know who or how to be?

....

....

....

....

As before, you may have developed negative cognitions, or thoughts, about yourself as a result of your early experiences. What might these be? Some examples may be "I'm not good enough" or "I'm incapable."

After you have identified what your negative thoughts are, how can you challenge those? What would you like to believe about yourself instead?

It is helpful to practice separating your past experiences from you current life. As you sort through these old memories, remember to ground yourself in the present.

You are no longer a toddler, and can learn to make healthy and independent decisions in your life.

✏️ Exercise:
VISUALIZATION — 1-3 TODDLERHOOD

To begin, start with three long, deep breaths. Allow yourself to settle into a comfortable position, sitting or lying down. Feel your limbs relax, and notice the relaxation moving into your core. Your heart slows and your breathing becomes steady.

Return now to the landscape of your life established in the previous visualization. Pay special attention to the details, letting them solidify in your mind's eye. What do you see, hear and smell? What do you feel, with your hands and feet? Notice the trees, bushes, flowers, water and anything else in the environment.

Imagine one of your earliest memories, from somewhere between 1 and 3 years old. If you don't remember anything from this time, choose something based on a story you've heard from family or mental snapshots you have. Select a time you were unhappy or when something happened that was painful to you.

As you begin, watch the painful scene unfold before you. What are you wearing? How is your hair cut or fixed? Notice how small you are compared to those around you. Pay special attention to the expression on your face.

As the scene plays out, where you are spanked or something is taken away, where you are scolded or dismissed, watch your inner child and the pain you experience. Maybe the time you're remembering you were abandoned by someone; notice all the details as your toddler self is upset.

As the scene ends, go to your toddler self. Take yourself aside, into another room or space where you can feel safe. Introduce yourself. Take time to comfort the little you.

> **I love you.**
> **You're safe with me, and I'll be with you always.**
> **I'll never leave you.**
> **You have every right to be angry, upset and scared.**
> **It's OK to be sad.**
> **It's not your fault; I'll help you learn about your world.**
> **I am you, and will always help you when you need me.**

Hug your toddler self and say "goodbye." Remind your younger you that you'll be back whenever needed before you turn and leave the room.

Now begin again, with the same scene, only you are now your toddler self. See all the same things in your environment, visualizing the smells, feelings and experiences of your little self. Relive the experience and allow yourself to hear the words of your loving adult self. Feel comforted having the attention and nurturing of a safe adult who knows how to meet your needs.

As you end this meditation, remember that you can use it whenever you feel abandoned, ashamed or confused. Allow the **positive feelings of being cared for** to continue with you as you move into your day.

PART 2: ELEMENTARY YEARS

"If you've told a child a thousand times and he still does not understand, then it is not the child who is the slow learner."

Walter Barbee

Crisis and trauma during this time of life is bewildering and frequently leads to confusion and lack of ability to have positive recall. Impairment in learning and creativity can greatly affect you for years. Relax and stay mindful through this process.

3-6 PRESCHOOL

Preschool time is when you started to get creative, asserting yourself more frequently and engaging people. The identity crisis to master is the development of initiative or guilt. Are you able to self-start, or do you feel inadequate on your own? Family relationships, beyond just Mom or your parents together, are the most important. You look to siblings for play, parents to engage in your make-believe, and family activities to support your creativity.

If your environment was nurturing and supportive, you likely have the ability to be on your own and initiate activity. You feel comfortable alone, and can engage with others. You are able to make decisions with relative ease and confidence.

If, however, your creativity was squelched, you may struggle in these areas. If your efforts to engage were met with criticism or disregard, you likely developed a sense of guilt. Your parents were possibly controlling or judgmental. If so, you may feel like a burden to others and will tend to be a follower rather than a leader.

What do you recall from this time in your life? There will be both positive and negative to recall, and I encourage you to do so below.

....
....
....
....

Were you in a preschool or at home? What do you know about how your time was spent?

....
....
....
....

Did you have things to play with, and a means to get creative? (This does not have to mean a lot of toys, but rather an environment in which learning and growing was promoted.)

....
....
....
....

Did people of all ages interact with you?

....
....
....
....

How were your sibling relationships?

....
....
....
....

Identify three examples in which your initiative was disregarded or criticized.

....
....
....
....

Now, remember three times where you were supported or encouraged to lead and plan.

....
....
....
....

The primary question to be answered at this time in your young life was whether or not it is OK for you to do, move and act. You were developing a sense of purpose, and the response by family was critical to the mastery of this task. How do you best answer that question now, as you reflect on your preschool years?

Based on how you responded to the previous question, how then do you view yourself?

....
....
....
....

What did you learn about your place in the world, given your preschool years experience?

....
....
....
....

How do you view the world? Is it a place where you feel comfortable? Can you make decisions and engage people in a meaningful, satisfying way? Is it painful and uncomfortable for you to interact with people?

....
....
....
....

What negative beliefs about yourself may have developed from the lessons learned? This may be "I'm stupid," "No one likes me" or "No one cares about me."

....

....

....

....

What about positive beliefs? Even if this time was challenging, you came through it with some lessons learned and skills developed. Perhaps "I'm resilient" or "I can take care of myself" fits. Explore what positives did happen, and spend some time reflecting on those.

....

....

....

....

Now challenge yourself to change those automatic negative thoughts and beliefs. Remember that you were a small child and had a limited amount of power. What kind of support or validation would your preschool self have benefited from? How can you nurture that part of yourself in the here and now?

....

....

....

....

✏️ Exercise:
VISUALIZATION — 3-6 PRESCHOOL

Begin with taking deep breaths as you get comfortable and relax into visualizing your life landscape. Find the path to the past, and follow it until you reach your preschool self. Remember a time when you were 3, 4, 5 or 6. Pick a time when you were unhappy or afraid.

How do you look? Notice your hair and your clothes. Are there toys around, some of your favorite things to play with? While you study yourself, remember the time you felt frightened or upset. Was it waking up alone, without a parent around? Was it the time your dad lost you at the mall? When your mom came home drunk and was scary? Maybe it was a bully kid at daycare.

As the memory unfolds, watch your preschool self. Notice the look on your face and the emotions as they play out in your body and expression. Do you cry or cringe? Tense up or back away? Watch your preschool self try to make sense of things that are too big to comprehend and understand. You are trying to make things right even though you are too little and don't yet have the skills.

When the scene ends, take your inner child by the hand and lead yourself into a safe and comfortable space, away from where you've just been. Tell yourself that you are from the future, and you have grown up able to take care of yourself. You are able to be the nurturing parent you needed.

Tell your preschool self you love her (or him).
I'm glad you're a girl (or boy).
You're special, and no one else is like you in the world.
You're doing your best, and this is not your fault.
It's OK to ask for things, and say "no."
You can ask me for anything.
You just don't have much power because you are so little.
You're good at thinking and imagining.

How is your preschool self understanding the situation? Try to get a sense of what your young self believes is going on. Is this shaping their view of themselves or the world, their lovability or safety? Because it is confusing, offer your preschooler an explanation for things that ensures they are not to blame. How does their reaction make sense in the situation? Help her or him see things with a positive angle on how they responded. Hug your inner child. Remind her/him you'll see them soon, and leave the room.

As before, change perspectives at this time and experience things from the perspective of your younger self. Allow yourself to truly experience the emotions you felt: shame, anger, confusion or fear. This is a difficult but critical part of the visualization working. Pay close attention to your adult protective self, really listening and knowing that you were not to blame. Notice how small you are, and realize the limited power you have at this age.

The next step is different than what you've done before. You are still your preschool self, although this time you are reliving the painful experience as if you have the knowledge already that things will be OK. It is as if you know the message from your adult self already, and understand what you were told: that you're OK, you will survive, and it's not your fault.

As you experience the scene, you feel less pain than before. Things are less intense. If you are comfortable, re-imagine yourself doing something differently. Change the memory; ask an adult for help if you are lost rather than sitting down and crying; listen to music and draw if you can hear your parents fighting. Remember that your brain doesn't care about the "truth"; it will respond emotionally to whatever you imagine.

However you approach this phase, do not blame yourself for not doing things differently. You did the best you could. Do not change what the people in your memory were doing, only alter your own actions. It's important to remember we have no impact on others' actions, even while imagining.

As you wrap up this exercise, take several long deep breaths. Return to this for any painful memories, working through each one mindfully and openly. This can also be helpful if you are feeling dependent, ashamed or guilty. Remember that those emotions can often be tied back to these developmental stages. Consider these visualizations before you jump to self-judgment or blame.

6-12 CHILDHOOD

Elementary school is a challenging time during which many lessons are learned and habits formed. The developmental task results in feeling a sense of industry, in which you are able to complete activities and get needs met, or inferiority, in which you end up doubting yourself.

School and your neighborhood play a strong role in how this skill is mastered. Teachers who are encouraging help to foster the sense of accomplishment you got from initiating a project and seeing it through to completion. Perhaps you played games with children in your neighborhood, making rules and engaging in a way that was enjoyed by everyone. Maybe team sports were an area in which you thrived.

Were you supported during this time in your childhood? Was your neighborhood a safe place to play and learn? How about school? Were you supported by teachers and able to ask for help when needed? Were you encouraged to figure things out in a way that was meaningful and validating or were you criticized for needing help? If you were not allowed to flourish independently, you may have begun to doubt your own ability. The result of this may be that you did not reach your full potential.

Recall this time in your childhood. What negative events may have happened in your elementary school years (first through fifth grade) that are impacting you now?

....
....
....
....

Now think of times that your independence was encouraged and you had pride in your accomplishments.

....
....
....
....

The big, existential question to answer is, "Can I make it in the world of people and things?" Do you have a general sense of competence, possibly stemming from school, sports or other activities? How do you view yourself? Are you proud of your achievements? Are you able to meet goals? What beliefs about you came from these years?

....
....
....
....

How about the world? Do you view it as an encouraging and supportive place in which to live and work? How did you view your world at that time; your school and neighborhood?

....
....
....
....

Because negative experiences during development can often lead to negative beliefs about ourselves, as we've seen, we want to continue to explore how this phase impacted your sense of self. What negative thoughts may have come from your early school years? "I'm not good enough," "I'm a failure" or "Nothing I do is good enough" may all fit.

....

....

....

....

Now, what positive beliefs do you have? Reflect on an accomplishment from this time and see what beliefs come up? "I am good enough" or "I can do it" could be positive beliefs to reinforce.

....

....

....

....

As you pull up the positive experiences and times during which you felt competent and encouraged, use the slow butterfly hug to help grow those good feelings. Remember that you are able to meet goals and successfully complete tasks. Let those positive sensations increase until they fill you up and you are able to see the negative from a different perspective.

VISUALIZATION — 6-12 CHILDHOOD

This follows the same pattern as previous visualizations. Get relaxed and return to your life landscape. Go to a place and time where you were any age 6 to 12. Maybe you were embarrassed at school or your dad didn't come to your big performance. Imagine all the elements of this memory, including how you looked, what your facial expression was, and how things felt at that time. Relive the painful memory from the perspective of your future, adult nurturing self. See your child self going through it all.

At the end, go to your child self. Take him or her into a safe place and tell yourself the things below in your own words. You can add or change things as they fit.

I love you.
The way you are is OK, at school and at home.
I'll stick up for you.
You can trust your feelings.
It's OK to feel afraid or disagree.
You can make your own decisions.
You're acting normally for your age.
How you dress is your business.

Now try to get a sense of how your child self is understanding and interpreting the event. Pay attention to how they are making sense of their place in the world as a result of this event. What does it mean in terms of lovability or control? Offer an explanation to your young self that relieves them of any blame. Provide a positive interpretation of their response.

Move into the scene again, this time from the point of view of your child self. Feel all the old, painful feelings while having the support of your adult self, as well. How does it feel to have a loving response from an adult? Next, relive the experience with the knowledge your adult self provided. You know that things are going to be OK, and you truly understand what your adult self was telling you. If you like, spend time changing how you reacted in the situation.

Wrap it up by giving yourself credit for doing this difficult work. Breathe and relax, knowing that you are healing your trauma and validating your school-age self and experiences. Use this exercise for any school memory that is still distressing and contributing to your negative thoughts. This is also a helpful visualization when you're feeling discouraged or incompetent.

PART 3: MIDDLE & HIGH SCHOOL YEARS

"Common sense is the collection of prejudices acquired by age 18."

Albert Einstein

Experiences that are common in adolescence form our view of the world and also cement our beliefs of limitations within ourselves. Be open to evaluating your experiences and perhaps new windows of opportunity will be opened.

12-18 ADOLESCENCE

Adolescence is a stressful time in the best of environments. The transition from childhood to adulthood is filled with learning opportunities and developmental tasks that can result in a lasting impact on your adult self. During this time, you are answering the question "Who am I?" and "What can I be?" These are really big and difficult questions, and this phase of life poses many challenges.

Did you have role models or people to look up to? What about peers? Social relationships take the place of family and neighborhood at this point in life. What information about yourself did you get from those close to you?

The mastery of this phase of life results in seeing yourself as unique and integrated. You understand who you are and what your values are. You know how you fit into your world.

If this time was traumatic or chaotic, you may not have developed a solid sense of identity. You may often experience confusion and doubt about who you *really* are. You likely were trying to think about the future and what possibilities it held. If that exploration was encouraged, you emerged into adulthood with purpose and identity. If your parents or environment were discouraging, it was likely that you finished high school with little plan for the future or understanding of your place in society.

This is not to say that you can't develop that now; we are simply exploring how circumstances at different phases influenced how your personality and world views developed.

What do you recall from adolescence? What kind of relationships did you have?

....
....
....
....

Who were your role models?

....
....
....
....

What activities were you interested in? Did you have any hobbies?

....
....
....
....

Who was your best friend?

....
....
....
....

Recall any negative memories from this time, particularly those that have to do with social relationships.

....
....
....
....

Now identify three positive memories from your adolescence. Nothing is too small to count!

....
....
....
....

Referring back to the big question, "Who am I?" — what is the answer? Do you know or have some idea? Brainstorm some ideas below.

What conclusions do you come to about yourself after considering your adolescence?

....
....
....
....

Do you have a perception of the world that stems from this time?

....
....
....
....

What did you learn about your place in the world from your high school years?

....
....
....
....

Chances are that you also established some negative thoughts about yourself during this time. If you had a history of not mastering the previous stages' developmental tasks, then these negative thoughts may have stuck. Perhaps "I'm a failure," "I'm unlovable" or "No one cares" relates to your experience. Write your negative thoughts below.

How about positive thoughts? What did you learn from high school that yielded positive self-beliefs? "I'm a good friend" or "I'm OK just as I am" are both possible examples.

What proof from your current life do you have that contradicts your old, negative self-belief? How can you challenge the negative cognitions from high school that are interfering with your adult relationships and social functioning?

....
....
....
....

How can you work to decrease a sense of confusion in your life and how you view yourself? Explore your values and use meditation to work toward an answer to the question, "Who am I?"

....
....
....
....

✏ Exercise:
VISUALIZATION — 12-18 ADOLESCENCE

This exercise begins like all the others. Imagine your life landscape. Go back to where you are between 12 and 18 years old. This time was likely full of events from which to choose. Maybe you rebelled against your parents, had conflicts at school with peers or teachers, fell in with the wrong crowd, or had strong sexual feelings beginning to develop.

Choose any painful memory to work with, and notice as many details from it as possible. Relax into your past, and get fully into the memories, emotions and sensations.

First, observe from your adult point of view. Notice how those around you are responding to you. As you play the memory all the way through, watch your adolescent self carefully. Once you are through it, take your adolescent self aside. Get somewhere safe and say to yourself the following things in your own words:

> **You can make healthy choices.**
> **You can experiment with sex safely.**
> **It is OK to disagree with your parents**
> **You can find someone to love.**
> **You can do something meaningful with your life.**
> **It's OK to feel confused and lonely.**
> **It's OK to be focused on yourself now.**
> **You have lots of ideas and thoughts about life.**
> **You're doing the best you can.**
> **Often you have no real choices in things.**
> **No matter how crazy things get, I'll be here for you.**

Find a way to explain things to your adolescent self that conveys it is not his or her fault. Try to find a way that positively interprets their behavior and choices. Again, allow yourself to feel the pain of the event fully, with your adult self there for support.

The second time, work through the memory with your adolescent self having the knowledge provided earlier. Maybe you change your behavior this time as well. Visualize yourself clearly knowing, internally, the above statements are true.

Break when you're done, breathing and stretching to return to the present moment and allow the effects of your visualization to take hold.

Repeat this exercise with any painful memories from your adolescence. Return to your adolescent inner child and this visualization any time, especially if you are struggling with issues related to sex or are in conflict with authority.

Moving Forward ...

Throughout your life, up until adolescence, you were a bystander, a child in a world of people with more power and control than you. The primary people in your life, particularly parents and later teachers, had significant influence on how you grew and developed your sense of self and the world. Broadly speaking, **who did or said what to you** to solidify your negative beliefs and self-image?

Now, as we move forward into adult phases of life and development, the question becomes **what have you done or said** to solidify these negative thoughts?

During adolescence and early adulthood, you may have unintentionally been reinforcing these negative developmental patterns. The challenge for your current self is to begin to identify what you have done to perpetuate the negative thoughts and stop carrying your trauma forward into life. It may be that you are successful in certain areas of life, and you have left trauma behind in those situations.

However, you may also be carrying it forward in other aspects. I often see this in relationships vs. careers. People are able to function well at work or school but have immense difficulty maintaining healthy and balanced relationships with peers or partners.

In domestic violence, there is an oft-referred to idea of the "wheel of control." Trauma often acts in a similar way for people, and this can be a helpful way to assess your current trauma responses.

What parts of your life do you feel out of control of or powerless over? Do you use emotional abuse or intimidation to get needs met? Are you out of control with your children or your finances? Do you isolate, minimize or blame others? All of these can mimic an abusive partner and be reflective of trauma and unmet developmental needs.

As you work through the final and adult phases of life and growth, consider the elements of this wheel. How are you carrying forward the impact of trauma in these areas?

PART 4: ADULTHOOD

"When one door closes, another opens; but we often look so long and so regretfully upon the closed door that we do not see the one that has opened for us."

Alexander Graham Bell

In this final section, you will explore how you developed intimacy in relationships. Learning to love and be loved is hard work for all of us and comes with many challenges. You will be asked to reflect on your most vulnerable questions of living, loving and moving forward.

19-40 YOUNG ADULTHOOD

Early adulthood typically refers to that time between graduation from high school and getting settled into a career, relationship, family, home, etc. During this phase, the most important relationships are those with friends and partners. This may be your current situation as you are completing this workbook, or maybe it was a time not so long ago. At this time, we share ourselves with people more intimately than we ever have. We are looking perhaps for someone to share our life with, other than those immediately related to us.

The task at hand is to develop intimacy. If this is not successfully mastered, a sense of isolation settles in. Success leads to comfortable relationships and a sense of commitment and safety. There is care and consideration within your relationships.

If you tend to avoid these types of relationships, or have not been able to develop them, you may experience loneliness or depression. If you fear commitment because of a previously unmet developmental need, the early adulthood time can be particularly difficult as peers get married and settle down.

What have been your experiences with romantic relationships?

....

....

....

....

Do you have close ties with peers or a partner?

....

....

....

....

What might be preventing this intimacy from developing?

....

....

....

....

Have you had any particularly upsetting relationship events?

....

....

....

....

Identify three negative events that have occurred during this time. If you are too young to have reached this phase, do you anticipate any struggles with developing intimacy? If so, consider those here.

....

....

....

....

Now consider your positive experiences in relationships. They don't have to be strictly romantic; if you feel a sense of intimacy with a friend, that counts. Don't discount yourself! What are examples of a time when you were close with someone and it felt good?

....

....

....

....

The existential question at hand is, "Can I love?"

Consider your examples from above. How would you answer this question? Do you have relationship proof of your ability to love and care for others? How about to receive love and affection? For some, this is more difficult than giving love. This may be due to embedded feelings of unworthiness or self-doubt. Can you commit to a relationship? Are you able to love?

- As you look at this time in your life, what do you learn about yourself?
- What kind of person are you in relationships?
- Where do you fit in the world of social relationships and commitment?
- Does your inability to develop intimacy or your feelings of isolation affect your view of the world?
- Based on the above reflection, what negative beliefs about yourself might have developed? For some, it may be "I'm unlovable" again or "I'm unworthy."

Now consider the positive. What positive beliefs do you have about yourself and your place in the world or relationships? "I can connect" or "I'm a good friend or partner" might fit. Challenge yourself to think of something positive that fits this category. This is a critical part of your healing from trauma!

How can you challenge any of the negative beliefs you've established? Consider where they have come from and how you can counter them with alternate evidence. Remember not to discount anything.

VISUALIZATION — 19-40 YOUNG ADULTHOOD

Begin this visualization in a comfortable position again. Imagine your life landscape and go back to your young adult self. This may or may not be very far down the path; and in fact, wherever you are in life, this can be helpful. Settle on a painful scene and watch how it unfolds. Allow yourself to experience the emotions associated and notice your bodily sensations as you watch.

Once it is complete, visit with your younger self. Let that part of you know that you will learn what you need to know in life.

You will learn to love and be loved.
You will make a difference in your world.
You can be a success.
You are doing the best you can.
You are acting normally for your age.
You often do not have choices.

Find a way to be compassionate to your young self. Find a new interpretation for your behavior and the event that is congruent with this compassion.

As before, return to the event with the perspective of your young adult self. Experience all the pain and frustration that you had then, only this time your older self is there for support and guidance. Hear what your future self has to say about things. Then revisit as your young adult self having all the knowledge and wisdom imparted by your older self. You have internalized the above messages and may choose to do things differently this time around.

Return to the present. Ground yourself in the here and now. Know that you can handle things in your adult life. Return to this visualization for whatever scenes need healing. This is also helpful for any time you feel confusion, particularly related to "adult" issues such as love, money or work.

40-65 MIDDLE ADULTHOOD

Most of your development has been completed by now. You have gone through the most intense periods of development, but that does not mean your work is done. The crisis at this stage is referred to as "generativity vs. self-absorption" or stagnation.

Mastery of this phase includes giving back to society, raising children and/or being productive at work and becoming involved in the community. If this stage is not navigated successfully, individuals feel unproductive and bored.

- Where are you in this phase? Do you have a career? Are you in school? Draw attention to your professional or work self.
- How about relationships and family? Are you raising children? How is that going?
- How involved are you in the community or social network of peers?
- How satisfied are you with these roles?

Do you have negative events in this phase of life? Remember that you may be carrying trauma forward in some or all of these areas. How does that show up?

....
....
....
....

What positive events or successes do you have? Promotions at work, good parenting moments, community involvement with a positive impact may all be examples.

....
....
....
....

The existential question is, "Can I make my life count?"

If "yes" is not your answer to this question, think about what life changes you might make to alter your answer.

What do you need to put in place in order to make it count? Maybe volunteering, returning to school, or changing jobs. If you are well into middle age, how have you made it count so far? If your response to this is not satisfactory to you, what changes can you make?

Remember that having a life of meaning does not mean the same thing for everyone. Do not judge yourself compared to others. Explore your values, read inspirational stories and meditate.

Find what is important to you and then live it.

Make choices every day that are congruent with your goal and not based on past trauma.

Once in adulthood, the negative and positive beliefs stem more from the past. However, there are events that may occur that reinforce those old beliefs.

Are there events that support old trauma-based negative thoughts?

....
....
....
....

What about events in your adult life that reinforce positive beliefs about yourself? What might these be?

....
....
....
....

How can you increase the opportunities in your life to grow and strengthen these positive beliefs?

....
....
....
....

Create a life of meaning every day by choosing your actions, relationships and thoughts wisely.

65+ SENIOR YEARS

During this time of life, individuals slow down, work less and reflect more on life. Accomplishments are contemplated, and if we view ourselves as successful, then we develop a sense of integrity. There are positive feelings toward our family development and professional experiences. A general sense of fulfillment and life satisfaction reflects a favorable outcome for this phase.

If you are in this stage, and this is not your experience, you may be feeling a sense of despair or hopelessness. It is not too late to change this, though!

If you are reading this book, you are in a position to create positive experiences and a sense of fulfillment in your life. Continue to challenge yourself to grow and change, explore your past trauma and how to contain it in the past, rendering it powerless over your current life.

If you are not yet in this phase of life, consider when you will be. How do you want to feel? What would you like to reflect on when you get older? Many individuals with trauma have a sense that they will not see their future.

Don't let despair or hopelessness take over. You have control in each moment to make a change, choose your actions and thoughts, and create a life worth living for yourself.

The existential question is, "Is it OK to have been me?"

What do you need in life to answer "yes" to this question? Below, identify ways in which you can create a reality where "yes" is the true response.

....
....
....
....

If you are already here, and the answer is not "yes," then what do you need to do differently? Remember, you are carrying your trauma forward and are the only one in control of putting it in the past for good. Your past no longer has control over you. How can you increase integrity and satisfaction?

....
....
....
....

In summary

How do your beliefs about yourself and the world impact you now? Which of those listed above have the most weight? Identify them below for further exploration:

....
....
....
....

How do you know they are true? Is there a possibility that these are simply myths you learned in a family where chaos and dysfunction ruled? As you consider these questions, remember to maintain a mindful stance. Stay present in the current moment, and merely observe your past; don't allow yourself to get swept up by it. Imagine that you are watching scenes on a television, or billboards on the highway as you drive. Be aware of your breathing, and notice other bodily sensations with gentle curiosity. Do not judge, and do not be hard on yourself if you need to take a break or come back to this activity at a later time. Use the space below to reflect on your thoughts.

....

....

....

....

....

....

....

Chapter 10

MEMORY TIMELINE

"Our duty is to preserve what the past has had to say for itself, and to say for ourselves what shall be true for the future."

John Ruskin

Being reflective and understanding how precious moments or terrifying moments can change your life forever can seem like an overwhelming task. This chapter will help make sense of these moments and how they define you. This insight will help you gain wisdom and take back emotional control.

This is another opportunity to explore how the past is interfering with the current. Use the previous pages to complete a timeline. Go at your own pace, and remember to take breaks and stay mindful. Most importantly, take care of yourself!

As you fill in the age and events that have occurred, remember that you are in the present moment, not the past traumatic events.

BY DOMINIK MARTIN

Anything might fit on this timeline; it doesn't have to be any particular kind of trauma or adverse life event. It can be any experience that interferes with your relationships, thoughts, feelings or self-image. It may be helpful to list these in chronological order to the best of your ability. Because of what we know about how memories are created and stored, it is often helpful to work through past events in the order they occurred.

Use the following worksheet to look at how the past may be impacting your life. How does not having trust mastered interfere with relationships now? Perhaps you struggled at middle school age, and the result is you end up being taken advantage of in current relationships because you feel inferior.

Refer back to the challenges you posed to the negative thoughts above. How can you use those to gain some control over your response to these negative events?

Practice accepting (not approving of!) the past. Use the butterfly hug and dual awareness. Remember, if at any time things get overwhelming, stop. It's OK to take your time in this process, and take care of yourself as you go. Consult your therapist as needed.

CREATE A MEMORY TIMELINE

Age	Distressing Event	Life Interference
Task	Belief About Yourself	Challenge to the Belief

Age	Distressing Event	Life Interference
Task	Belief About Yourself	Challenge to the Belief

Age	Distressing Event	Life Interference
Task	Belief About Yourself	Challenge to the Belief

Age	Distressing Event	Life Interference
Task	Belief About Yourself	Challenge to the Belief

Age	Distressing Event	Life Interference
Task	Belief About Yourself	Challenge to the Belief

Age	Distressing Event	Life Interference
Task	Belief About Yourself	Challenge to the Belief

Age	Distressing Event	Life Interference
Task	Belief About Yourself	Challenge to the Belief

Age	Distressing Event	Life Interference
Task	Belief About Yourself	Challenge to the Belief

Age	Distressing Event	Life Interference
Task	Belief About Yourself	Challenge to the Belief

Age	Distressing Event	Life Interference
Task	Belief About Yourself	Challenge to the Belief

Chapter 11

ANXIOUS THOUGHTS & COGNITIVE DISTORTIONS

"A healthy mind has an easy breath."

Author unknown

Anxiety and worry rob us from enjoying life. They distort our awareness which brings on useless suffering. In this chapter, you will learn ways to calm your anxieties and reassure yourself.

OVERCOMING YOUR NEGATIVE THOUGHTS

Now that you have explored your past, what negative thoughts are you carrying forward, into your relationships? You have identified where the negative thought patterns originated, and now you are going to learn how to decrease the power they have over you.

Human tendency is to overestimate the chance something bad will happen, especially when we are already anxious or traumatized. It is important to understand the actual probability of a particular negative event occurring and to develop a plan for coping. This will reduce the power of the hold negative thoughts have on you.

ESTIMATING THE REAL ODDS

- Write down the anxiety-provoking thought, and then objectively estimate the real odds of that actually happening, without being judgmental.
- Assign a percentage to that likelihood. This helps to create an accurate perspective.
- Remember that your anxious thought is not a fact nor certainty; it is merely a guess.
- If this event has occurred before, how often? How frequently does reality deliver life as negatively as you anticipate it ahead of time?
- What evidence supports that the feared event will not happen? What positives have you put in place to protect yourself? What have you done to reduce your vulnerability factors?
- Identify what alternative possibilities there are. What could happen besides what you fear?

DECATASTROPHIZING & COPING

- What would be the actual impact if this terrible thing happened? Remember that we tend to overestimate; things are usually not as bad as we'd envisioned. The consequences are typically shorter, less intense, and have fewer effects later than we'd predicted.
- What would you do if it did happen? What skills have you mastered that could help reduce the consequences? How can you manage your emotions despite the event? What can you do to increase the positive influences coming into your life and increase balance?
- Remind yourself that there are ways to cope with everything, regardless of its intensity. You have coped with significant events already, and remembering that finding a way to healthily manage stress is empowering and healing.
- What would your healthiest self do? Go back to the conference table. Who is in charge of your coping? Who do you want to be?
- Things change all the time. **Feelings are not facts, they are not fatal, and they are not final.** Remember that when emotions seem to overwhelm you.

COMMON ERRORS IN THINKING

Thinking errors occur in everyone. They are the irrational, illogical or unhelpful thoughts that can become automatic responses to stress, emotions and events. If you can start to identify what cognitive distortions you experience, you are more able to change them and have a more adaptive thought pattern. Do not automatically believe everything you think!

Below are some common thinking errors. Are there vulnerability factors that might increase your chances of thinking these ways?

It is likely that you have moved away from Wise Mind if you are experiencing errors in thinking.

If so, in what direction have you gone? Unrelenting crisis? Active passivity? Apparent competence? Inhibited emotion? Exploring the dialectical dilemmas and vulnerability factors can help you understand yourself better, and therefore begin to change.

ALL OR NOTHING, BLACK AND WHITE THINKING

Idealization or devaluation of people falls into this category. Have you eliminated someone from your life based on a minor indiscretion? Do you fall in love hard and fast? Does this lead to a sense of ongoing crisis in your life?

....
....
....
....

What makes you vulnerable to this kind of thinking? How can you move toward Wise Mind when it happens?

....
....
....
....

"Shoulding" — Trying to motivate yourself through conditional language like "should" or "must." This tends to result in guilt, anger, frustration and resentment. Challenge yourself to change this language: Instead of "I shouldn't feel this way," consider what information you might learn from your emotions.

Is there something that needs to be addressed in a relationship? If the feeling is uncomfortable, can you address it safely and learn to tolerate it?

Remember to maintain a non-judgmental stance while looking at your "shoulds."

....
....
....
....

What makes you vulnerable to this kind of thinking? How can you move toward Wise Mind when it happens?

....
....
....
....

MENTAL FILTER

Selecting one element or a single event and focusing all your energy on that, while ignoring the bigger picture. This can happen especially when you have moved into unrelenting crisis. One small aspect takes on a life of its own, and you no longer consider all the information.

What makes you vulnerable to this kind of thinking? How can you move toward Wise Mind when it happens?

....
....
....
....

DISCOUNTING THE POSITIVE

Rejection of any positive aspect of an experience and coming up with reasons why they don't count. This is also being willful. Have you ever minimized something to "Anyone would have done the same thing" or "It was no big deal"?

....
....
....
....

What makes you vulnerable to this kind of thinking? How can you move toward Wise Mind when it happens?

....
....
....
....

EMOTIONAL REASONING

Thinking that because you feel a certain way, it must be accurate and a reflection of reality. Remember that **feelings are not facts**. Do you ever experience anxiety or fear and assume that you must be in some kind of danger? This is emotional reasoning.

....
....
....
....

What makes you vulnerable to this kind of thinking? How can you move toward Wise Mind when it happens?

....
....
....
....

OVERGENERALIZATION

Taking one negative outcome and applying it to all areas of your life. After a rejection, or unreturned phone call, you think, "This *always* happens" or "I'll *never* have a relationship."

....
....
....
....

What makes you vulnerable to this kind of thinking? How can you move toward Wise Mind when it happens?

....
....
....
....

JUMPING TO CONCLUSIONS (AKA "MIND-READING" AND "FORTUNE-TELLING")

This is when you assume you know another person's intentions, attitudes, beliefs or other mental activity. This may show up as assuming that someone is judging you or thinking negatively about you. "Fortune-telling" is assuming that you know what another person is going to do or say before they do it, "I know you're not going to like this, but ..."

....
....
....
....

What makes you vulnerable to this kind of thinking? How can you move toward Wise Mind when it happens?

....
....
....
....

PERSONALIZATION AND BLAME

These present a dialectical dilemma: personalization occurs when you assume sole responsibility for something, ignoring other contributing factors; blame is the opposite. You hold someone else responsible without considering your own impact on the situation. If you find yourself in active passivity often, you may be employing one of these cognitive distortions.

....

....

....

....

What makes you vulnerable to this kind of thinking? How can you move toward Wise Mind when it happens?

....

....

....

....

LABELING

Labeling relates back to the story we tell about ourselves and/or others that then shapes our experiences. If you've adopted the label "I'm unlovable," it is easy to view the world through that lens, and attend only to the events that prove that. Labeling impacts our view of reality and can negatively influence relationships and self-esteem.

....

....

....

....

What makes you vulnerable to this kind of thinking? How can you move toward Wise Mind when it happens?

....

....

....

....

Here I have listed some common negative beliefs. Check those that apply to you, remembering that these may have been influenced by developmental traumas revealed in your earlier work. Then, list experiences that confirm that belief.

O I'm unlovable

O I'm a failure

O I'm a bad person

O I deserve bad things to happen

O I'm unworthy

Confirming experiences

....

....

....

....

Human beings like to be right. This is true no matter what the subject; people enjoy being right about things.

Because of this, we tend to pay more attention to the evidence around us that supports our belief. If this is a negative, then we are more inclined to notice events that confirm that.

For example, if at your core, you believe that you are not lovable, you may engage in behavior that reinforces this notion. You may have sex with people who don't care about you or start fights with friends who then abandon you. Both of these behaviors reinforce the idea "I'm unlovable."

What experiences do you create that confirm your negative beliefs? As a child, things were done *to you*. You did not have control. As an adult, you are now in charge of either reinforcing or dissolving those negative beliefs.

What can you do to change those negative beliefs?

How can you change your behavior as well? What new and positive belief can you identify and reinforce?

The following page can help you change your patterns of thinking. Use these and apply to your own current negative thoughts.

WAYS TO CHANGE YOUR THINKING

Identify the distortions: Identify your automatic thoughts and the cognitive errors used. Develop a more rational response.

Cost Benefit Analysis: List the advantages and disadvantages of holding onto the thoughts, feelings or behavior.

Examine the Evidence: Instead of believing the negative thoughts you have are true, look for proof.

Survey Method: Do a survey to find out if your thoughts and attitudes are realistic. Ask your support people.

Double Standard Technique: Ask yourself if you would feel the same way if it were a friend in the same situations. Talk to yourself as you would your friend about your feelings and behavior.

Vertical Arrow Technique: Instead of disputing your negative thoughts, ask yourself, "If this were true, why would it be upsetting to me? What would it mean?" Try to get to your underlying beliefs.

Shades of Gray Technique: Instead of looking at things in black and white terms, try to see shades of gray. If you are having trouble at your job, ask yourself what your strengths and weaknesses are instead of seeing yourself as a failure or unable to do the job.

Define Terms Technique: When you catch yourself labeling, ask what do I really mean by this? An example may be calling yourself a total loser. Ask, "What is a total loser?" Surely you will find that what you are thinking is not accurate.

Semantic Method: This works well when you are labeling and using "should" statements. An example might be when you have made a mistake and you start to beat yourself up by saying things like, "I am such a jerk, I should not have made that mistake, I should have known better." Instead, say things like, "It would have been preferable if I had not made that mistake, however, everybody makes mistakes. What can I learn from this?"

Reattribution: Instead of blaming yourself completely for a problem, look for other factors that have contributed to it. "What caused the problem?" "What was my role and what were the other factors involved?" Move into a problem-solving mode.

Accepting Paradox: All of the above methods assume that what you are thinking is illogical. Instead of defending your self-criticism, find some truth in it and accept it. Ask yourself, "What is really true? Can I accept that I have some flaws and have made some mistakes? What can I learn from them? What is my next step?" This is also the opportunity for **radical acceptance**.

Chapter 12

WHO'S IN THERE?

"He who knows others is wise; he who knows himself is enlightened."

Lao Tzu

Trusting and knowing yourself allows you to find true happiness. Oftentimes people lack insight into themselves, leading them to be taken advantage of by others. This over-dependence on others leaves you vulnerable. Learning who you are and what has guided your life is truly rewarding.

NESTING DOLLS AND YOU

Consider Russian nesting dolls. Each previous size is contained within a bigger doll.

This is similar to the experiences we have as a baby, which do not simply go away because we get bigger and older. Each experience is contained within us.

The same is true for events throughout development. Our previous experiences, both positive and negative, are stored in body and mind. If some of these events are traumatic, their impact can be felt for a lifetime. Remember what ACEs you may have experienced.

It is important to note, too, that these events do not have to be headline-making tragedies, although they could be.

So often, I hear clients say, "It wasn't *that* bad." "My childhood was nothing compared to hers," and other invalidating and discounting comments. It is critical that you do not perpetuate your own traumatic experience by invalidating yourself.

Events can have a lasting effect no matter their initial intensity or the intention of the people involved.

Perhaps your mom was in the hospital for a few weeks when you were an infant. Maybe you were lost briefly at the mall. What might you have learned if your family never spent recreational time together?

All of these situations can influence how we view ourselves, the world, and our place in it.

What has happened that could have been ineffectively stored in your memory networks?

....
....
....
....
....
....
....
....

What are the stages in which you experienced traumatic life events or development may have been hindered?

....
....
....
....
....
....
....
....

How might this be impacting relationships in your adult life?

....
....
....
....
....
....
....
....

INTERNAL FAMILY SYSTEMS OR EGO STATES

This exercise can help you explore past experiences and how they may be influencing your current life. It involves considering all the work you have done up to this point.

Look at the times in your life where you endured traumatic experiences. Consider the age you were, the beliefs you developed as a result, and the generational patterns your family tree illustrated.

Look also at the way you respond to stress in your day-to-day life. How do you react? How old do you feel in those reactions? Do you ever have the sense that you are a younger version of yourself?

It is not uncommon for past response patterns to be activated when a traumatic or stressful event occurs that is linked in our memory network to a past situation.

For example, when you sense that someone is mad at you, it may remind you of being yelled at as a child, and you may shrink and retreat in an attempt to keep yourself safe. As a child, that may have kept you safe from physical abuse. Now, though, it may interfere with getting your needs met by those people in your life who care about you.

Make a list of situations in which you feel as though you are not your Wise Mind self. Are there situations where you feel a particular emotion take over? How old does it make you feel? How big a part of yourself is that part?

Describe the part in terms of size and intensity. Maybe it is a small or weak-feeling part, or perhaps it is very strong and seems to take over when activated. Get to know the different parts of yourself using a curious and nonjudgmental stance. Remember, each of these parts has or does serve a purpose for you.

Situation	Emotion	Age	Part Description
....	....	....	....
....	....	....	....
....	....	....	....
....	....	....	....
....	....	....	....
....	....	....	....
....	....	....	....
....	....	....	....

✏ Exercise:
MAP OUT YOUR PARTS OF SELF

Imagine a classroom in which there are many different students. Each has their own set of needs, demands, expectations and comfort zones. The teacher is in charge of trying to meet the needs of each individual student, as well as ensure they learn what has been deemed necessary.

Use the space on the following page to map out these parts of yourself. The list might be helpful in starting to identify different aspects of you. It is a starting point; use the words that fit for you. Unlike a classroom, where each child is an individual person, in this exercise, each part is a part of your true core self.

There are likely parts that are bigger and stronger than others, and in your visual representation, those "students" would be bigger and more defined. Other parts, perhaps stemming from younger experiences, will be small, nervous and timid. Use these characteristics to draw each part of yourself in your classroom. Although there are many parts, the teacher is in charge of the entire classroom. The teacher is like your Wise Mind. Turn to it for guidance and support. Know that part of you knows best, and will carefully consider options in order to make the best decision.

There will be times when a part of you takes over that is not the teacher. When this happens, support that part of yourself. Let yourself know that you have this under control, and that things are very safe for that part of you here.

This may be very scary. Or it may be an exciting exercise to do. No matter what your experience, take your time and complete the page thoughtfully, adding to it as necessary. There may be a part that dominates because it is protecting or masking other parts. If the teacher is absent or not in control, parts may have had to step in over time to get things done or merely survive.

This was necessary.

There could be parts you don't like or aren't comfortable with. I encourage you to get close to those parts, too. Try and nurture them, and understand how they came to be. Acknowledge that all parts have a role, and have been important in your life. If, though, the teacher is not the most present part, you will likely have difficulty attaching and having authentic relationships.

It is not required that you have good drawing skills. Rather, the most important thing is that you create a representation that is meaningful and helpful to you. This may mean that in each chair is a shape in a different color. They don't have to be accurate drawings of people. Do what works.

Examples:	Happy	Caring	Promiscuous
Loving	Smart	Talented	Purposeful
Scared	Worried	Unique	Honest
Patient	Helpful	Depressed	Graceful
Kind	Strong	Bold	Articulate
Funny	Eccentric	Expressive	Artistic
Bossy	Anxious	Strong	
Athletic	Earthy	Alert	

Questions:

- Are there parts that are particularly active? Perhaps you routinely feel angry and frustrated. Give that angry part a big area. Notice how it seems to take over the smaller parts.
- How does it feel to have certain parts and emotions dominate the "conversation?" Imagine all the parts need to collaborate under the supervision of your **Wise Mind self.** How does it work?
- Are there parts that seem to be sitting back, unable to let their voices be heard?
- Maybe there is a part in the corner that feels especially young or vulnerable? How can your **Wise Mind self** manage this "meeting" in order to let all your parts be heard?
- Remember, because each part has played a role in your life, it is important to acknowledge and validate them. It may be that their service is no longer needed, in which case, gently encourage that part to sit and observe rather than engage in the dialogue.
- What do they need to feel safe and secure?
- How can you talk to these parts in a nurturing and validating way? Use the space below to write out some sentences that you can refer back to when certain parts take charge that are better left on the sideline. Remember to use positive language and make it appropriate to that part's age.

....
....
....
....
....
....
....
....
....
....
....

Chapter 13

LETTING GO

"Everybody's got a past. The past does not equal the future unless you live there."

Tony Robbins

You survived your childhood and now it is time to take charge of your life. You can no longer be a passive bystander in your life waiting for someone to notice you and love you. You must give the love you did not receive; you must give in an optimistic way and be patient for the returns. The return will be given back to you. If others do not give it back, you will receive it within your soul. You will no longer be afraid of life. You will no longer lay awake full of self-hatred and wishing for death. You can learn to let the past go.

It is completely normal to reach a point of feeling full of emotions and thoughts. When this happens, a skillful approach can help mindfully assess what needs to be expressed and what needs to be let go of.

As we've discussed and you've learned previously, this act of discernment is a critical piece of healing and recovery from Borderline Personality Disorder. There are times when it is important to let those in your life know what is on your mind and not keep it bottled up. Similarly, there are times when it is best to accept and move forward without sharing.

You will find a few options for learning to let go of these thoughts and feelings described below. Take some time to practice each, and use what is of the most benefit.

BY PAUL JARVIS

RELAX YOUR BODY

It is difficult to be upset if your body is relaxed. There are a number of breathing techniques, as well as progressive relaxation, that can be used to help you achieve this relaxation.

- Breathe slowly and deeply as you visualize the tension leaving your body with each breath.
- Inhale and exhale the same number of counts (in for three, out for three). As you do, imagine your breath going in and out of your heart while recalling or thinking of things that give you an appreciative or loving, grateful feeling. If you are inspired by this approach, we encourage you to further explore HeartMath (heartmath.org).
- Practice "bottom of the breath" breathing. Inhale slowly, then exhale, pausing before you inhale again. In this space between breaths, you may experience easier access to your Wise Mind or spiritual core.

- Recall or imagine a very happy, peaceful scene. For this exercise, you will likely be best served by establishing a scene at a time when you are still and mindful that will be easier to recall in stressful moments.
- Deliberately relax certain trigger points, such as jaw muscles, your pelvic floor, hand, or the third eye between your eyebrows.
- Try to systematically place your attention gently on each major part of your body, starting with your feet and working up to your head. If it helps, think of a phrase like "relax" as you move up. An alternate approach to this is to tense your muscles for about five seconds before then completely relaxing.

RELEASE PAINFUL FEELINGS

- Remember that suffering comes from the non-acceptance of pain. There will be times in your life when you will need to help painful feelings move through you, and resist holding onto them or attempting to suppress them.
- Safely vent. Write a letter about how you really feel that you'll destroy after it's written; maybe burn it in a ritualistic fire, scattering the ashes and letting the emotions go as you do. Tell a trusted friend, with the clear intention of getting rid of it rather than getting more worked up. Yell out loud in the shower, underwater or while driving a car (stay safe while driving, though!).
- Give a color and texture to your feelings, sense them draining out of your body, perhaps through your fingers and toes.
- Exhale the feelings with each breath, while intentionally breathing in something positive (exhale anxiety, inhale peace).
- Visualize your emotions being swept away by standing in a cool and refreshing stream on a calm and sunny day.
- Imagine placing your feelings in a jar or bottle and tossing them in the river to be carried out to sea, or on a rocket that will be burned up by the sun.

SAY "GOODBYE" TO NEGATIVE THOUGHTS

Get on your own side and argue the case against the negative feelings, limiting or inaccurate thoughts, beliefs, expectations and assumptions. Think it or write it down.

What are these thoughts or beliefs from the past that are no longer serving a purpose? Use the space below to write them down, then list three ways in which they are totally wrong. You may refer back to the section on thinking errors in previous chapter for additional guidance. Structure and determination will make this most helpful.

Negative Thought   **Arguments Against**

....

....

....

....

....

....

LETTING GO THROUGH BENEFICIAL SERVICE TO OTHERS

Always know that giving is as good as receiving. If you did not receive the love and nurturing as a child needed to master these developmental stages, it is not too late to internalize the pieces missing and create a loving, connected life for yourself today.

In this exercise, you will learn to create social support in your life and overcome the fears set in place in childhood.

First ask yourself, "How can I be supportive now?"

Challenge yourself to be yourself around others and offer to give someone the support you are wanting. (Fear may keep you from reaching out. Be brave.) It is the ability to take risks that help give us the competence to move forward.

Ideas for giving:
- Challenge yourself to volunteer with children, the elderly, at hospitals or any community center.
- Nurture a pet; adopt a dog or cat from the shelter.
- Parent your children by mindfully giving daily in a way you were neglected.
- If you are really going to enjoy life, you must plan out your day and your relationships.
- Offer kindness to a friend, relative or neighbor.

Reflection Questions:
What did you learn about yourself?

....
....
....
....

If your parents did this giving exercise, how would it have changed things for you and your parents? What would you learn about yourself?

....
....
....
....

One of the ways I am going to give what I did not receive today is?

....
....
....
....

Chapter 14

WHAT'S IMPORTANT & LIVING ACCORDINGLY

"You have to believe there are kisses and laughs and risks worth taking."

David Levithan

In this next chapter, you will define your best self. Answer these questions:
"What do you want out of life?" and "What are your values?" Create a vision
for yourself and realize, with time and awareness, you have the power to create
the life you dream of achieving.

IDENTIFYING VALUES
& LIVING CONGRUENTLY

In order to move through trauma and build the life you want, you must know what is important to you. What motivates your choices?

Now that you are **free from your past**, you have the space to identify and **choose your own priorities.**

This may be difficult. It may feel unnatural to consider some of these, and your family may have different values than those you now select.

As you examine this list, pay special attention to your **Wise Mind**. What is your bodily response to each as you review the list?

Highlight those that speak to you, and make a separate list of the most important.

Use this list to outline ways in which you currently live in congruence and unity with these values.

If you struggle to identify places where these values exist, how might you change that? Can you think of opportunities in your life where you might incorporate value-based decisions and choices?

This will help you build mastery and increase your sense of self and well-being, as well as decrease incongruence and subsequent distress.

✏ Exercise:

IDENTIFYING YOUR VALUES

Highlight the words that speak to you about the life you want to have.

Abundance	Availability	Compassion
Acceptance	Awareness	Competence
Accessibility	Awe	Competition
Accomplishment	Balance	Completion
Accountability	Beauty	Composure
Accuracy	Being the best	Concentration
Achievement	Belonging	Confidence
Acknowledgement	Benevolence	Conformity
Activeness	Bliss	Congruency
Adaptability	Boldness	Connection
Adoration	Bravery	Consciousness
Adroitness	Brilliance	Conservation
Advancement	Buoyancy	Consistency
Adventure	Calmness	Contentment
Affection	Camaraderie	Continuity
Affluence	Candor	Contribution
Aggressiveness	Capability	Control
Agility	Care	Conviction
Alertness	Carefulness	Conviviality
Altruism	Celebrity	Coolness
Amazement	Certainty	Cooperation
Ambition	Challenge	Cordiality
Amusement	Change	Correctness
Anticipation	Charity	Country
Appreciation	Charm	Courage
Approachability	Chastity	Courtesy
Approval	Cheerfulness	Craftiness
Art	Clarity	Creativity
Articulacy	Cleanliness	Credibility
Artistry	Clear-mindedness	Cunning
Assertiveness	Cleverness	Curiosity
Assurance	Closeness	Daring
Attentiveness	Comfort	Decisiveness
Attractiveness	Commitment	Decorum
Audacity	Community	Deference

Delight

Dependability

Depth

Desire

Determination

Devotion

Devoutness

Dexterity

Dignity

Diligence

Direction

Directness

Discipline

Discovery

Discretion

Diversity

Dominance

Dreaming

Drive

Duty

Dynamism

Eagerness

Ease

Economy

Ecstasy

Education

Effectiveness

Efficiency

Elation

Elegance

Empathy

Encouragement

Endurance

Energy

Enjoyment

Entertainment

Enthusiasm

Environmentalism

Ethics

Euphoria

Excellence

Excitement

Exhilaration

Expectancy

Expediency

Experience

Expertise

Exploration

Expressiveness

Extravagance

Extroversion

Exuberance

Fairness

Faith

Fame

Family

Fascination

Fashion

Fearlessness

Ferocity

Fidelity

Fierceness

Financial independence

Firmness

Fitness

Flexibility

Flow

Fluency

Focus

Fortitude

Frankness

Freedom

Friendliness

Friendship

Frugality

Fun

Gallantry

Generosity

Gentility

Giving

Grace

Gratitude

Gregariousness

Growth

Guidance

Happiness

Harmony

Health

Heart

Helpfulness

Heroism

Holiness

Honesty

Honor

Hopefulness

Hospitality

Humility

Humor

Hygiene

Imagination

Impact

Impartiality

Independence

Individuality

Industry

Influence

Ingenuity

Inquisitiveness

Insightfulness

Inspiration

Integrity

Intellect

Intelligence

Intensity

Intimacy

Intrepidness

Introspection

Introversion

Intuition

Intuitiveness

Inventiveness

Investing

Involvement

Joy	Outlandishness	Refinement
Judiciousness	Outrageousness	Reflection
Justice	Partnership	Relaxation
Keenness	Patience	Reliability
Kindness	Passion	Relief
Knowledge	Peace	Religiousness
Leadership	Perceptiveness	Reputation
Learning	Perfection	Resilience
Liberation	Perkiness	Resolution
Liberty	Perseverance	Resolve
Lightness	Persistence	Resourcefulness
Liveliness	Persuasiveness	Respect
Logic	Philanthropy	Responsibility
Longevity	Piety	Rest
Love	Playfulness	Restraint
Loyalty	Pleasantness	Reverence
Majesty	Pleasure	Richness
Making a difference	Poise	Rigor
Marriage	Polish	Sacredness
Mastery	Popularity	Sacrifice
Maturity	Potency	Sagacity
Meaning	Power	Saintliness
Meekness	Practicality	Sanguinity
Mellowness	Pragmatism	Satisfaction
Meticulousness	Precision	Science
Mindfulness	Preparedness	Security
Modesty	Presence	Self-control
Motivation	Pride	Selflessness
Mysteriousness	Privacy	Self-reliance
Nature	Proactivity	Self-respect
Neatness	Professionalism	Sensitivity
Nerve	Prosperity	Sensuality
Noncomformity	Prudence	Serenity
Obedience	Punctuality	Service
Open-mindedness	Purity	Sexiness
Openness	Rationality	Sexuality
Optimism	Realism	Sharing
Order	Reason	Shrewdness
Organization	Reasonableness	Significance
Originality	Recognition	Silence
Outdoors	Recreation	Silliness

Simplicity
Sincerity
Skillfulness
Solidarity
Solitude
Sophistication
Soundness
Speed
Spirit
Spirituality
Spontaneity
Spunk
Stability
Status
Stealth
Stillness
Strength
Structure
Success
Support
Supremacy
Surprise
Sympathy
Synergy
Teaching
Teamwork
Temperance
Thankfulness
Thoroughness
Thoughtfulness
Thrift
Tidiness
Timeliness
Traditionalism
Tranquility
Transcendence
Trust
Trustworthiness
Truth
Understanding
Unflappability

Uniqueness
Unity
Usefulness
Utility
Valor
Variety
Victory
Vigor
Virtue
Vision
Vitality
Vivacity
Volunteering
Warmheartedness
Warmth
Watchfulness
Wealth
Willfulness
Willingness
Winning
Wisdom
Wittiness
Wonder
Worthiness
Youthfulness
Zeal

PRIORITIZE YOUR VALUES

Create your top 10 list of the values that speak to you:

....

....

....

....

....

....

....

....

....

....

....

....

Ways I live them and new ways to try:

....

....

....

....

....

....

....

....

....

....

....

....

HOW TO MAINTAIN YOUR VALUES AND GOODWILL

Once you have identified the values motivating your behavior and life, it is important to explore how living accordingly will enhance your life and what the cost of forfeiting them might be.

Although it will certainly be challenging at times, maintaining goodwill toward yourself and others will dramatically increase your overall sense of well-being.

When you communicate effectively and maintain a sense of self separate from others, you are not overwhelming to others or to yourself. This can be one way to motivate yourself to work hard at maintaining your values.

Use the next sections to help identify exactly why you have chosen to do this hard work on your past and live with intention. Really consider what the benefits are to being in the moment and resolving your past trauma.

This is what we refer to as "goodwill." It is a commitment to keep trying; a commitment to continue working toward your goals.

Even when you fall off the wagon.

REFLECT

On the benefits to yourself of living with purpose. Think of your **life worth living and maintaining your self-respect**. What are ways you might remind yourself of this?

....
....
....

What are the benefits to others of you living intentionally from your values? Really try to have a positive emotional connection to these benefits, not just a passing thought.

....
....
....

Consider the costs to yourself and others if you don't maintain your values or goodwill.

....
....
....

Allow yourself to feel an appropriate degree of remorse for not maintaining your values or living with virtue. Make the necessary repairs to your relationships.

....
....
....

COMMIT

Privately make a commitment or vow to yourself or your higher power.

....
....
....
....

Declare your intentions publicly, and commit to yourself and others to maintain your value-oriented stance and goodwill. Make a promise to a significant person that you will stick to your commitment unless you specifically state that you have changed the commitment.

....
....
....
....

Get a little angry at the distractions that arise in your mind that divert you from your purpose.

....
....
....
....

Write a letter of intention to yourself to be read if your commitment starts to fade.

....
....
....
....

If it works for you, imagine a teacher, friend, or group — or possibly a particular teaching, spirit or God, who stands for the same values and purposes that you want to live by — and do what they advise.

....
....
....
....

In general, surrender to your highest virtue and purpose. Let go of willfulness and self-righteousness. Give yourself over to your values.

....

....

....

....

SET GOALS

Do things that remind you of your highest intention. Write some key objectives in the morning and journal in the evening, reflecting on your congruence with your values that day.

....

....

....

....

Post intentions, affirmations, inspiring quotes from others or motivating pictures where you will see them regularly. Identify your highest values to yourself before sleep and upon waking.

....

....

....

....

Attend with intention to the benefits of your virtues and purposes. Authentically experience these benefits so that you will naturally move in that direction in the future.

....

....

....

....

Set your values and purpose in life ahead of your mind. Let your values direct you.

....

....

....

....

Seek good company. Surround yourself with supportive friends and seek inspiration from mentors and teachers. Spend time in like-minded communities and participate routinely.

....
....
....
....

Create opportunity. Go to bed earlier, meditate in the morning, or do whatever will help put yourself in the place to do the right thing.

....
....
....
....

Establish routines that embody your value and purpose. Say prayers, volunteer regularly, or do yoga for 10 minutes each evening. Weave these routines into your daily life so they are easy to maintain and the people in your life expect you to do them.

....
....
....
....

Remove temptations. Change the things that can interfere with your ability to maintain your goals and values.

....
....
....
....

When feelings and desires to stray from your commitment arise, just notice them. It is not necessary to act on every thought that comes through.

....
....
....
....

As a general rule, do activities that increase your will. Try concentration exercises, intense physical activity, exercise or doing one thing each day that goes against a tendency in yourself that you're working to change. What will you change?

....

....

....

....

TAKE THINGS ONE DAY AT A TIME

Make a promise to yourself to stick with your goals for an allotted time, then reevaluate. What works? What doesn't? How has a particular practice benefited you or the people in your life? Mindfully choose what you would like to maintain and/or change about your routines.

Chapter 15

YOUR RELATIONSHIP ROLE

"Shared joy is double joy, shared sorrow is half a sorrow."

Swedish Proverb

Do you feel detached from relationships? Do you distrust others? Do you frequently come unglued in relationships and punish others quickly if you feel let down? Traumas can cause reaction for as long as you hold the negative thoughts to be true and for as long as you act on these negative assumptions and self-blame. In the coming pages, you will understand your role in moving forward from the harmful reactions in relationships and learn ways to prevent them from continuing.

CONNECTION WITHOUT CHAOS

It is likely that you have identified in the previous pages some kind of relationship as part of your values. For most of us, relationships serve a vital role in our daily lives and overall satisfaction. It is also likely that relationships have been challenging, and even detrimental, to your wellness at times. Because of this, it may be difficult to recognize and maintain healthy relationships. Often, this has to do with intensity.

We know from the earlier exercises on "family of origin" and "patterns of relating" that the degree of intensity may have been confusing at best. Perhaps your parents reacted very strongly to things that were minor, and did not respond appropriately when something significant happened. This confusion with intensity leads to difficulty in relationships that can be profound.

In this section, we will discuss how to tailor your intensity to match the situation and relationship.

THE FOUNDATION OF THIS IS TO BE MINDFUL

It is critical to maintain awareness of how past events are impacting your current functioning and how that influences your relationships.

We will look at what assumptions you make in relationships. Are there automatic thoughts that interfere with you actively and mindfully participating in relationships? There may be roles in relationships, that you or someone else played previously, that are being reenacted now despite being dysfunctional or destructive.

Let's begin with some exploration of roles in relationships.

What role in relationships do you have?

....
....
....

Do you find that there are patterns to your relationships?

....
....
....

Is intensity ever an issue? Do people tell you that you're overreacting? Do they shy away from you or make comments about how you might react?

....
....
....

What do you do in the face of conflict? How does it make you feel to consider someone being mad or disappointed?

....

....

....

How disturbing is it if someone is upset? How do you handle that upset?

....

....

....

One of the primary problems individuals have in relationships is responding to conflict or upset in a manner that is disproportionate and perhaps extreme.

Have you threatened suicide when someone does not reciprocate an invitation? Have you cut someone out of your life because you've felt slighted by them? Consider a time when you may have "overreacted" to an event. What did that look like and how did the other person respond?

It is important to accurately identify the level of intensity required in a particular situation. When we approach situations with the appropriate degree of intensity, we bring people closer, build a sense of mastery, and maintain healthy relationships.

This is what establishes equal footing in relationships as well; people feel energized and engaged by relationships in which they are on an equal playing field. There isn't a sense of being taken advantage of, manipulated or disrespected.

Are you considering what the appropriate degree of intensity is in a particular interaction?

This is sometimes a difficult task. Take some time to identify what intensity is required in whatever situation you're in. I've provided an example to help you assess.

- 10 - I'll kill you or myself if I don't get my way.
- 8 - I'll divorce you if I don't get what I want.
- 7 - I'll give up on this relationship.
- 5 - I will say something about my concern and balance without considering their view.
- 3 - I drop hints but don't directly ask for what I want.
- 1 - I'll do and say nothing, choosing instead to please the other person.

In order to have successful relationships that are congruent with your values, it is important that you maintain an appropriate degree of intensity.

Do you tend toward being over- or under-intense in relationships?

For individuals who have experienced a traumatic or chaotic childhood, assessing intensity can be particularly difficult.

When that is the case, people tend to develop a particularly high tolerance for intensity and drama. If you have a high tolerance for stress and intensity, then you may feel a sense of emptiness or boredom when things are more tame and less intense.

This is a dangerous place to be because the tendency can be to create the drama and intensity that is missing.

In order to address this urge to create drama, you must **remain mindful** and hold close the values you've identified. This means addressing conflict as it arises. Use the skills that you've acquired through this process to notice what is a remnant from the past and what is a reaction to the current situation.

Is there a situation in which you know your intensity was out of proportion to the event?

....

....

....

What skills can you employ to tolerate waiting, or the urge to engage, when Wise Mind suggests it would be better not to?

....

....

....

How do you decrease your vulnerability to emotional mind, as well?

....

....

....

There will undoubtedly be times when you do not have a choice or a desirable option. Sometimes there is nothing to do but accept reality or be miserable. What will you choose?

RADICAL ACCEPTANCE

Radical acceptance is the bold and sometimes painful or difficult act of accepting what *is*. It is the extreme, or radical, acceptance of reality. This *does not* mean that you have to approve or like what has happened. It is not condoning bad or abusive behavior. It is, though, acknowledging what has happened in your past, either to you or by you. It is not an excuse to withdraw or become passive. It is permission to feel and grieve and experience your emotions, cultivating mindfulness and presence in the moment necessary for living life fully.

Radical acceptance is a critical piece of learning how to tolerate distress. There are simply things we cannot change. This applies to past trauma, as well as more mundane events like getting a speeding ticket or losing a favorite sweater. When we recall these events, and there is still significant emotional and/or physical distress, there is an opportunity to practice radical acceptance. The goal is not to forget what's happened, forgive perpetrators or live in denial. Rather, radical acceptance is the path to **emotional freedom**. When you accept what is, and do not carry it forward, you are giving yourself the freedom and space to heal and **live the life you choose**.

What do you need to accept? What part of your reality do you struggle to accept?

....
....
....

There are limitations to the future, but you only need to accept those that are realistic. Be honest with yourself and use your Wise Mind in this practice. What factual limitations are present?

....
....
....

You may be tempted to try and accept that "you're hopeless" or "doomed to be alone" but those are not based on observable information. Perhaps that has been the pattern in the past, but you cannot accept a future that has not occurred. You have the option to do things differently, therefore creating different results.

....
....
....

You may struggle to accept reality because you do not have the skills or the emotions are too intense. You may believe that if you do, you are minimizing the situation or creating the possibility for it to happen again. These are both tricks of the trauma, and you can learn to tame them with practice. Resisting reality does not change it, and will only serve to increase suffering.

What emotions may interfere with you accepting reality?

....
....
....

When you recall events that have happened that you struggle to accept, what do you experience in your body? What are the physical messages that you receive? Take a moment to think of something that is difficult to accept, and pay special attention to your body. Note what comes up.

....
....
....

Remind yourself that there are causes for everything. Reality occurred the way it did based on an innumerable number of events occurring prior, many of which likely had nothing to do with you. Consider how other people's lives have influenced them just as you did for yourself. What additional causes might you consider when thinking about your painful reality?

....
....
....

Combine thinking of these events with practicing some of the mindfulness exercises you've learned. While breathing and maintaining an open and curious stance, bring up images of what you're struggling with. Imagine yourself as open to whatever has happened, knowing that you can accept reality without losing yourself or giving in to strong detrimental urges.

What was this experience like for you? What might be helpful to increase your willingness or ability to accept reality? Is there still something blocking you?

....

....

....

Remember that life is worth living, even with pain in it. There is no way to eliminate pain altogether, nor would it work to do so. We need all emotions in order to experience life fully and participate actively. However, pain does not need to mean suffering. If you are suffering, it is likely that you have not accepted some piece of reality.

Chapter 16

SEEING GOODNESS IN OTHERS

"Make finding the good in others a priority."

Zig Ziglar

You will learn to see the good in those around you and hopefully have the same

returned to you!

Actively seeking the good qualities in others — strengths, good intentions, talents, values — can have many benefits.

This can help improve and maintain positive relationships with people. It can also bring out the best in others. When we see the positive in other people, it encourages them to "raise the bar" and interact with us accordingly.

You are also shaping your mind to attend to the good, something that you may not be used to doing. Others will appreciate this, and will have the positive experience of being seen with kindness.

A large part of this exercise involves **setting intentions**.

- When I wake up, I will look for the good qualities in at least one person. This encourages mindful observation and increases the time spent in **Wise Mind**.
- When you meet someone, pay special attention to their good qualities. Of course, they will have problematic qualities also, as we all do. We get to choose where we place our attention, though, so **choose wisely**.
- Reflect on the **lovingkindness meditation** that follows. Remember that other people also wish to be strong and healthy, and feel safe and protected. Notice how your intention of seeing good guides your choices as you interact with people, as well as how they respond to being treated with kindness.

Who do you need to see the good in? **Maybe the place to start is within yourself**. Challenge yourself as you feel comfortable to see the good in others.

....
....
....
....

Chapter 17

LOVINGKINDNESS MEDITATION

Kudos! You have reached the final chapter in this journey of transformation and healing. On the following page, you will find the lovingkindness meditation, which is a powerful meditative practice that can help you achieve your goals of self-acceptance and successful relationships.

BY YAIR HAZOUT

As you strive to implement all the practices from this workbook, remember that you get to choose where you place your attention. Although it may seem difficult at times, with practice, altering your perspective will get easier.

We are ending this workbook on notes of **radical acceptance, seeing goodness** and **lovingkindness** because of their intense potential for integration and healing.

However, these are also challenging concepts.

Persist in your practice, always remembering there is a way out of suffering.

In the long run, you will reap the rewards that come from forging this positive new path.

Today, congratulate yourself on the completion of this workbook.

You have shown true commitment on your path to wellness and have established habits that will not only support a lifetime of active participation, but also promote effective emotional engagement.

Continue to cultivate your power within as you **embrace yourself, accept yourself** and ultimately **love yourself**.

Worksheet:
LOVINGKINDNESS MEDITATION

A lovingkindness meditation is designed to increase your feelings of well-being and unconditional love and affection toward all beings. You may also hear this referred to as metta meditation. It will increase your love for yourself, as well as help you release judgment and condemnation of others. Your sense of connection and open-heartedness will increase, and you will become calm if you are upset or angry.

Sit comfortably, and allow your mind and body to settle. Now, begin the recitations.

For Yourself: **May I be safe and protected. May I be peaceful and happy. May I be healthy and strong. May I experience well-being.**

Continue repeating this as long as you wish, encouraging feelings of really wishing these things for yourself. If you want, you can end here; or, you can continue by offering lovingkindness to others.

For a Friend: **May he or she be safe and protected. May he or she be peaceful and happy. May he or she be healthy and strong. May he or she experience well-being.**

As above, you can end here, or continue to wish lovingkindness to a loved one. Additionally, in some practices it is encouraged to offer lovingkindness to someone with whom the relationship is strained in an effort to release that tension. Try this once you have practiced lovingkindness enough to be strong in your intention and not get filled with negative feelings or thoughts when using it for difficult people.

For a Loved One or Challenging Person: **May he or she be safe and protected. May he or she be peaceful and happy. May he or she be healthy and strong. May he or she experience well-being.**

When you are finished, offer to all beings the feelings of love, compassion, friendliness and openness you are having.

For all Beings: **May you be safe and protected. May you be peaceful and happy. May you be healthy and strong. May you experience well-being.**

References

Astrachan-Fletcher, Ellan, and Maslar, Michael. 2009. *The Dialectical Behavior Therapy Skills Workbook for Bulimia.* Oakland, CA: New Harbinger Publications, Inc.

Brach, Tara. 2003. *Radical Acceptance, Embracing Your Life With The Heart of a Buddha.* New York: Bantam Dell, A Division of Random House, Inc.

Dryden, Windy, and Raymond DiGiuseppe. 1990. *A Primer on Rational-Emotive Therapy.* Champaign, IL: Research Press.

Ellis, Albert. 1994. *Reason and Emotion in Psychotherapy.* New York: Birch Press Lane.

Forgash, Carol, and Copeley, Margaret. 2008. *Healing The Heart Of Trauma and Dissociation with EMDR and Ego State Therapy.* New York: Springer Publishing Company, LLC.

Freyd, J. J. (1997). *II. Violations of Power, Adaptive Blindness and Betrayal Trauma Theory.* Feminism & Psychology 7:22-32

Gonzalez, Anabel and Mosquera, Dolores. 2012. *EMDR and Dissociation: The Progressive Approach.* Anabel Gonzalez &Dolores Mosquera.

Goleman, Daniel. 1995. *Emotional Intelligence.* New York: Bantam.

Gottman, John, and Nan Silver. 1994. *Why Marriages Succeed or Fail.* New York: Fireside. 1999. *The Seven Principles for Making Marriage Work.* New York: Three Rivers Press.

Greenberg, Leslie, and Susan M. Johnson. 1988. *Emotionally Focused Therapy for Couples.* New York: Guilford.

Greenberg, Leslie, and Sandra Paivio. 1997. *Working with Emotions in Psychotherapy.* New York: Guilford Press.

Harvey, Pat, and Penzo, Jeanine. 2009. *Parenting a Child Who Has Intense Emotions.* Oakland, CA: New Harbinger Publications, Inc.

Herman, Judith L. (1992). *Complex PTSD: A syndrome in survivors of prolonged and repeated truama 5.*

Herman, Judith L. (1997). *Trauma and Recovery: The Aftermath of Violence.* Basic Books.

Kabat-Zinn, Jon. 1994. *Wherever You Go, There You Are.* New York: Hyperion.

Lazarus, Richard. 1991. *Emotion and Adaptation.* New York: Oxford University Press.
Linehan, Marsha. 1993a. *Cognitive-Behavioral Treatment of Borderline Personality Disorder.* New York: Guilford.
1993b. *Skills Training Manual for Treating Borderline Personality Disorder.* New York: Guilford.

Gottman, John. 1997. *Raising an Emotionally Intelligent Child.* New York: Fireside.

Greenberg, Leslie, and J. Pascual-Leone. 1995. *A dialectical constructivist approach to experiential change.* In Robert Neimeyer and Michael Mahoney, *Constructivism in Psychotherapy.* Washington, D.C.: APA Press.

Izard, Carroll. 1977. *Human Emotions.* New York: Plenum 1991. The Psychology of Emotions. New York: Plenum

Jacobson, Edmund. 1967. *The Biology of Emotions*. Springfield, IL: Charles C. Thomas

Kovecses, Zoltan. 1990. *Emotion Concepts*. New York: Springer-Verlag.

Lazarus, Richard, and Bernice Lazarus. 1994. *Passion and Reason: Making Sense of Our Emotions*. Washington, D.C.: APA Press

Niedenthal, Paula, and Shinobu Kitayama, eds. 1994. *The Heart's Eye: Emotional Influence in Perception and Attention*. San Diego: Academic Press.

Schmidt, Shirley Jean. 2009. *The Developmental Needs Meeting Strategy, An Ego State for Healing Adults with Childhood Trauma and Attachment Wounds*. Texas: DNMS Institute, LLC.

Shapiro, Francine. 2012. *Getting Past Your Past, Taking Control of Your Life With Self-Help Techniques From EMDR Therapy*. New york: Rodale.

Shapiro, Robin. 2005. *EMDR Solutions, Pathways to Healing*. New York: W.W. Norton & Company, Inc.

Siegel, Daniel J. 2010. *The Mindful Therapist, A clinical Guide to Mindsight and Neural Intergration*. New York: Mind Your Mind, Inc.

Siegel, Daniel J. 2011. *Mindsight, The New Science of Personal Transformation*. New York: Bantam Books Trade Paperbacks.

Spradlin, Scott. 2003. *Don't Let Your Emotions Run Your Life*. Oakland, CA: New Harbinger Publications, Inc.

Strongman, Ken. 1996. *The Psychology of Emotion: Theories of Emotion in Perspective*. New York: John Wiley.

Tibbitts, Amy. 2013. *You Untangled, A DBT Skills Workbook, Practical Tools To Manage Your Life*. Lilac Center.

Tomkins, Silvan, and Carroll Izard, eds. 1965. *Affect, Cognition, and Personality* (4th ed.). New York: Springer Publishing.

Traue, Harald, and James Pennebakes, eds. 1993. *Emotion, Inhibition, and Health*. Gottingen, Germany: Hogrefe & Huber

Van Dijk, Sheri. 2009. *The Dialectical Behavior Therapy Skills Workbook for Bipolar Disorder*. Oakland, CA: New Harbinger Publications, Inc.

www.ingramcontent.com/pod-product-compliance
Lightning Source LLC
Chambersburg PA
CBHW080556090426
42735CB00016B/3256